something
to prove

To Carrie

something
to prove

A Daughter's Journey to
Fulfill a Father's Legacy

A MEMOIR

Warmest Regards,

Yvonne S. Thornton, MD

with Anita Bartholomew

Yvonne S. Thornton, M.D.

March 22, 2022

Parrhesia Publishing

Published by Parrhesia Publishing
Division of Dryst, Incorporated
201-570-8181
Fax: 201-836-4199
Dryst.com@ludlowseminars.org

Library of Congress Cataloging-in-Publication Data has been applied for. Printed in the United States of America

ISBN-13: 978-0-57858-342-6

DEDICATION

To Shearwood —
My husband, my champion, my love

AUTHOR'S NOTE

*Patients' names and certain other identifying
characteristics have been changed to protect their privacy.*

TABLE OF CONTENTS

preface

IN 1995, MY FIRST memoir, *The Ditchdigger's Daughters,* was published by a small publishing house. Despite its unceremonious debut into the world of literature, it struck a chord with readers. Those who read it told their friends about it, and those friends told other friends, until pretty soon, they'd made it a national bestseller. Oprah Winfrey even featured my family's story on her television show. In 1997, *The Ditchdigger's Daughters* was adapted into an award-winning TV movie.

To this day, I still get letters and e-mail from readers newly introduced to my family's story, telling me how they were inspired by it. Let me quote from just three of the thousand or more I've received over the years:

From a single mother, juggling parenthood and a career:

"There are days when I feel overwhelmed just providing for one little girl and I got so much inspiration from your mother and father. There are quotes from your book that I will remember for the rest of my life."

preface

From a father in Maryland:

"As parents of a daughter, Robyn, 15, and a son, Robert, 12, we are trying to instill in them the same thirst for education and a strong moral character that your parents and my parents thought were vital… Our daughter has already decided that she wants to pursue a career in medicine and become a pediatrician. We are encouraging both our children to be the best that they can be."

From a nurse-practitioner in Georgia:

"I can relate to a lot of the trials that your family endured. Your father was such a wise man and it seemed that a lot of the things he said pertained to me. My self-esteem and self-worth were at an all-time low until I realized that I'm not in this struggle alone."

FOR THE PAST FIFTEEN years, many of these readers have asked me to write another book. This new book, *Something To Prove,* was born out of those requests.

But first, for those who are unfamiliar with *The Ditchdigger's Daughters,* let me tell you a bit about it. The book chronicled my parents' life story, centering on my father, Donald Thornton, a man of great wisdom but limited schooling. A child of the Great Depression, Daddy fought in World War II, married my mother, and by the age of 28, was the father of five girls and no boys.

Like parents everywhere, he wanted his children to have a better life. He struggled to provide for his wife and daughters.

His dream, which fueled our lives, was for all of his daughters to become physicians—a very lofty dream, considering that we lived in the housing projects of New Jersey. But my mother and father knew that education would propel us out of the projects and into the mainstream of life. He and my mother knew we had to go to schools on the better side of town.

So, with $200 he'd saved up, he bought a lot at a tax auction, and built our house himself, stone-by-stone, with my mother serving as his hod-carrier. On a parallel track, music came into our lives in the form of a saxophone followed by an interest in forming an all-girl family band. Once Daddy realized that we were good enough to be paid as professional musicians, he booked us for dances at colleges up and down the East Coast. The money we earned helped pay our college tuition. For thirteen years, The Thornton Sisters performed on the weekends and studied during the week. Despite our musical success, Daddy still wanted us all to become doctors. He spoke of the day that each of us would each be called "Dr. Thornton."

There were some setbacks in realizing his dream, but I did become the first physician in our family. That seemingly unreachable accomplishment inspired my younger sisters and motivated my older sisters to follow suit.

My parents' story was one of determination and strategic planning. My story has been one of a grateful daughter trying to keep my parents' memory alive and appreciating them for the lessons they taught me.

And now, I invite you to come along for the rest of my journey in *Something to Prove,* a book that begins where *The Ditchdigger's Daughters* left off, in the early 1980s, as I balanced a new career in the challenging world of academic medicine while being a wife and raising two energetic toddlers.

I hope you will take away from this new book its most important message, passed down from my parents to me, and from me to my own children:

With hard work, determination, and education, we *can* achieve anything.

—Yvonne S. Thornton, MD, MPH

chapter one

The Sub-Basement and the Glass Ceiling

New York Hospital–Cornell Medical Center
Early 1980s

"I knew in medicine, right, you'd always be respected.
When a man is sick, he doesn't look to see what color
you are, he wants to be made well."
　　　　　　　　　　　　—DONALD THORNTON

"COME TO THE HOSPITAL if your water breaks or if anything else goes wrong," I always told my patients. "We'll take care of you, even if you're not in labor."

Not all of them listened.

Mary Paulsen hadn't listened. Mary, pregnant with her first child, was a zaftig woman in her early 30s, full of life, and strong-willed. Her water had broken two days earlier but she'd had no contractions and so, against doctor's orders (mine), she just

1

stayed home. It wasn't until she felt feverish that she decided to come in to the Cornell Medical Center in Manhattan where I was the Director of Clinical Services for the Lying-In Hospital.

I could see right away that she had an infection of the membranes and the uterus, a potentially dangerous situation for both the mother and her baby. I started Mary on antibiotics. Then, I induced labor.

Everything went smoothly at first. She was two centimeters dilated, four centimeters … fully dilated. We moved her into the delivery room, the anesthesiologist administered the epidural—an anesthetic, delivered through a catheter near the spine, that deadens the pain of labor but doesn't put the patient to sleep—and soon after, Mary delivered her baby.

"It's a boy!"

I asked if she wanted to put him to her breast but Mary said she was too tired. As I handed the baby off to the delivery room nurse, I noticed that he smelled a little strange, probably because of his mother's infection. The nurse cooed as she placed him in an incubator. We sent the baby boy off to the nursery with the circulating nurse, where the pediatrician declared him healthy.

We were done, except for delivering the placenta. Or so I thought.

Usually, the placenta follows the baby right out but it can take up to thirty minutes. The clock ticked—twenty-five minutes, thirty minutes. Nothing happened.

"The placenta's just a little bit stubborn," I joked. But, in the back of my mind, I was thinking, *Please, God, don't let this be a placenta accreta.*

The Sub-Basement and the Glass Ceiling

Placenta accreta is a relatively rare and potentially fatal condition. It happens when the placenta attaches itself too deeply into the wall of the uterus, and it can cause complications.

"Get me more IV fluids," I said, and called for some Pitocin, an intravenous medicine that causes the uterine muscles to contract. I also told the nurse to get me an elbow-length glove so I could go in and remove the placenta manually, if necessary.

But a moment later, the placenta came out. I examined it to be sure it was intact. If it weren't, I'd have to remove any remaining chunks from the uterus. It looked like everything was there.

Relieved, I turned back to Mary to tell her we were ready to send her to the recovery room.

But Mary was still bleeding.

It's normal to see a little blood after the placenta is delivered, but nothing like this. This was the Red Sea.

Something was very wrong. I grabbed a speculum and checked. No lacerations to the vagina, no apparent rupture anywhere. Yet, the packing I had put in a moment before was soaked with blood. The uterus should spring back immediately after delivery to something very close to the firm, hard ball it was before pregnancy, literally shrinking from the size of a fat Halloween pumpkin to about the size of a pear. When that happens, it's as if the uterus becomes its own tourniquet; it clamps off the arteries pumping that blood. But if the uterus doesn't tighten down after delivery, then it's like an open wound. A pint of blood per minute goes through the uterus. A pregnant woman's body has, at most, twelve pints of blood. That meant that, in Mary, as much as a pint of blood a minute was gushing out of her arteries.

3

something to prove

As an obstetrician, Board-certified in maternal-fetal medicine, I was well-trained in managing complicated pregnancies. It was my specialty. But when something goes wrong in the delivery room, no matter how expert your training, the risks are great. A hundred years ago, one woman in one hundred died during delivery. Modern medicine has reduced those deaths to less than one in ten thousand. Even with all our modern medical techniques and knowledge though, childbirth is not risk-free. Complications in childbirth are the eleventh leading cause of death in women between the ages of fifteen and forty-four. And when women die in childbirth, it's most often because of hemorrhage.

What could be causing Mary's bleeding? I went through a checklist in my head. Could part of the placenta still be lodged inside?

"Get me a banjo curette," I called to the nurse and used the surgical instrument to scrape the walls of the uterine lining.

Everything was clean. And Mary was still bleeding.

Whether it was because the infection had caused a reaction or because something else was in play, Mother Nature had thrown us a curveball. About five minutes had passed since I'd delivered the placenta, and Mary's uterus—which should have firmed up and shut off the arterial gusher—had only about as much muscle tone as Great Grandma's flabby upper arms.

Mary complained that she felt lightheaded. Her pulse raced to 120 beats per minute. She was going into shock. We were losing her.

"Move her into the OR," I yelled, feeling dread. Only once had one of my maternal patients died. It had been a long time before, when I was chief resident at Roosevelt Hospital, but I could still picture every awful moment in my mind. It was July 19, 1976, and her name was Jazmin Rivas. She had been only 19 years old. Something that no one could have foreseen interfered with blood clotting after delivery.

I got the call at 3:14 a.m. I had been at home, across the street, in our twenty-fourth-floor apartment on West 59th Street, but I slept in my white coat, just in case there was an emergency. So when they called and told me that Jazmin Rivas was hemorrhaging, I was ready to go—I didn't even wait for the elevator. I flew down those twenty-four flights of stairs and got to the hospital in less than five minutes.

It didn't matter. We tried everything and we couldn't stop the bleeding. I watched her die on the table.

Later, in an autopsy, the medical examiner determined that amniotic cells had broken off and lodged in the young mother's lung, setting off this bizarre anti-clotting reaction.

Nothing at the time could have saved Jazmin Rivas. I knew that and yet I swore to myself, never again. Some things are out of the obstetrician's control, but from then on I was even more obsessive than I'd been before and whatever I could control, I did. Whatever I could prepare for in advance, I prepared for. I had always been determined to be the most careful, conservative obstetrician on the planet, and after Jazmin's death I was more so. I couldn't bear losing another patient.

Yet, here I was, close to losing Mary.

I had one important stop to make as I raced from the delivery room to the operating room. It's good that I had no time to think about it because it was painful. Out in the waiting room was Mary's husband, a big, happy smile on his face. He was a small, skinny guy with a full beard whose wife had probably far outweighed him even before she became pregnant. All he knew was that he had just become the father to a healthy baby boy. I had to bring him down to earth now and explain the situation.

"She's continuing to bleed," I said. "I have to go in. I want to see if I can tie off some arteries that feed into the uterus." I told him it was a serious situation and it would take a while before we knew the outcome. We might have to remove her uterus. I didn't want to do that but would do so if it were the only way to save her life.

As he absorbed all that, I stuck a clipboard under his nose. "We need to have this consent form signed."

In seconds, I watched his expression cycle through every emotion from elation at being a new dad to fear and despair that he might lose his wife. But he signed the form. And I followed Mary into the OR to scrub.

The whole gurney was filled with blood. I had the nurse call down to the blood bank for four pints. Mary was in shock and not fully conscious but I heard her mumble my name so I explained as we prepped that I had to go in, not knowing how much of what I said she could hear, let alone comprehend.

There was no time for niceties, and the prep was taking too long. "Give me the goddamned scalpel," I snapped, and made an incision from her belly button down to her pubis.

In the delivery room, I had tried to massage the uterus externally to encourage it to contract, but sometimes you have to go in and literally put the uterus between your hands and massage and massage until the little muscles get their memory back and function again. That was what I was doing now and it wasn't working any better. We had to find another way to stop the bleeding. I had my assistant take over massage while I went in to tie off one of the larger arteries that feeds into the uterus. I clamped it shut. And still, Mary bled.

"It's 60 over palp," said the anesthesiologist. Normal blood pressure is 120 over 80. Palp means that the second number is barely audible.

"It's 40 over palp."

"We're going to have to remove the uterus," I said. My heart sank at the thought. This was a young woman. She'd just given birth to her first child. If I performed an emergency hysterectomy, there would be no second child. If I didn't, she might have only minutes to live.

Before I took that irreversible step though, I wanted to make one more attempt to stop the hemorrhage. It would involve a more difficult procedure, one I'd performed only twice before, tying off an artery that's deep into the pelvis and surrounded by all sorts of other very vital organs.

Time was running out. I moved the bowel and carefully made my way around the ureter. There it was, pumping red. I tied off the artery. The bleeding reduced almost immediately to a trickle.

That was it. I realized I was soaked to the skin with perspiration even in the chill of the operating room. There were no high-fives, no shouts of success, just an exhausted team silently feeling relief at having saved a life.

And, from me at least, a quick silent prayer of thanks

because, no matter how well trained or experienced I was, I knew that I'd had a little extra help in the OR that day.

I HAD COME TO the New York Hospital–Cornell Medical Center in August of 1982 after serving for three years with the military at the National Naval Medical Center in Bethesda, Maryland. Volunteering to join the military hadn't been my idea. My big, darling bear of a husband, Shearwood J. McClelland, an orthopedic surgeon, said that we should give something back to the country that had given us so much. I could see that the military would have a great need for Shearwood's skills. But what use would the military have for a specialist like me?

Double Board-certified in both obstetrics and perinatology, also known as maternal-fetal medicine, doctors like me are typically thought of as über-obstetricians who consult on complex pregnancies such as multiple births or cases where the baby is known to have a defect that requires special care. A perinatologist would be called in if, for example, an ultrasound showed an abnormality in the fetus that needed to be managed, or if the mother developed diabetes or a pulmonary embolism.

I couldn't see where someone with my training would fit with battleships and submarines. What I hadn't considered, though, was that the wives of the sailors and Marines filling up those submarines and battleships showed their husbands how much they'd been missed when the ships docked at home after a six-month tour of duty. Talk about a baby boom! The Navy kept me plenty busy.

Shearwood and I might have renewed our commissions after our three-year tour except for a close call that nearly sent me to the Persian Gulf. It was during the Iran hostage crisis, and the Navy needed another surgeon to deal with potential battlefield injuries. Never mind that I wasn't that kind of a surgeon, or that I had two tiny children—Woody, then 3, and Kimberly, barely a year old. My commanding officer said they could quickly teach me gut surgery. My family obligations were of no interest to the military. I was in the Navy and where they sent us, we had to go.

Lucky for everyone, the hostages were released in January of 1981, and my proposed tour of duty in the Persian Gulf was canceled.

After that, Shearwood agreed that we should resign our commissions at the end of our first tour of duty—we were both lieutenant commanders—and apply for academic positions at teaching hospitals in the civilian world.

I KNEW THAT MY résumé looked impressive. I had worked hard to get where I was. After attending medical school at Columbia University College of Physicians and Surgeons, and completing my residency in obstetrics and gynecology at New York's Roosevelt Hospital, I'd gone on to complete a postdoctoral fellowship in maternal-fetal medicine at Columbia. And while on active duty for three years in the Navy, I passed my Boards for certification in maternal-fetal medicine. I was the first African-American woman to gain that Board certification. Of course, my résumé didn't mention ethnicity, just my educational and career accomplishments, which may have been why I got such an odd greeting when I arrived at The New York Hospital–Cornell Medical Center, which had hired me, sight unseen, as its new director of clinical services for the Lying-In hospital.

As a black woman, I've experienced racism and sexism throughout my life and believed I was prepared to deal with it whenever I had to. Even so, I will never forget that first week after I reported to my new job.

IN THE THREE YEARS at the National Naval Medical Center in Bethesda I'd become accustomed to working where everything was gleaming and state-of-the-art. Whatever the latest technology was, we were among the first to have it at Bethesda. So I was taken aback, at first, by how antiquated Cornell's buildings were.

The New York Lying-In building was across from the ER, past a cobblestone courtyard. The lobby was dark and drab. It was the second oldest hospital in the United States, and looked it.

I found my way to the Obstetrics and Gynecology department on the main floor. This area, too, looked like something from another time. The secretarial pool was in the center and the doctors' offices were lined up along either side. I didn't know which of those offices would be mine but I could already tell that it would definitely need cheering up.

Still, Cornell was one of the most prestigious teaching hospitals in the country—it was where the PAP smear originated—and I was thrilled that I was about to become part of its faculty. I was starting as an assistant professor, but with my credentials and a lot of hard work I could imagine myself one day rising in this prestigious old bastion to full professor.

The Sub-Basement and the Glass Ceiling

Everyone's dreams of success are different. For my father, a ditchdigger with only a tenth-grade education, success meant raising his five daughters to become doctors; and, indeed, three of us fulfilled that dream. One of my older sisters, Jeanette, had first become a psychologist and then later became an MD like me; and a younger sister, Linda, was a prosthodontic oral surgeon.

For a number of doctors I knew, success meant a private practice and a seven-figure income. That was never my goal. To me, success meant teaching medical students and residents, and rising to the top in the world of academia. I knew the pay would never come close to what my friends in private practice earned, but it didn't matter; this was where I wanted to make my mark.

I also had two little children. Working regular hours meant I could be with them as much as possible. Much as I loved delivering babies, I never wanted to have to miss my own child's school recital or a game or a parent-teacher's conference. The path that I'd chosen would allow me to share my knowledge as a teacher, and consult with the obstetricians in private practice. Those doctors were the ones who made the big bucks, but they were also the ones who answered those three o'clock in the morning phone calls telling them to hustle to the hospital because someone's bundle of joy wasn't going to wait until dawn to make his debut appearance in the world.

THAT FIRST DAY AT Cornell, I walked up to the reception desk in the Obstetrics and Gynecology department and introduced myself to one of the secretaries. "Hello, I'm Dr. Thornton.

I have a meeting with Dr. Druzin." I explained that I was the new staff doctor in maternal-fetal medicine and could see her do a double-take before she told me to have a seat and wait. Conversations around us stopped. Several other people walking by perked up as I announced myself. They weren't rude but it was clear I'd caught everyone by surprise. It didn't take much analysis to figure out why.

I was the only black person in sight.

This was 1982, when a woman obstetrician was still a rarity; a black woman obstetrician was even more unusual. A black woman with a subspecialty in maternal-fetal medicine was unique indeed. But the vibe I was getting had less to do with being a relatively exotic addition than with not belonging.

I felt uncomfortable, but I'd spent my younger years on stage with my sisters and mother. The Thornton Sisters played every weekend—that was how my parents were able to scrape together the money to put us all through college. I'd learned how to put on a happy face for the audience no matter what I was feeling inside, and that's what I did as I awaited Dr. Druzin.

He came out a few minutes later. I didn't know it then, but I learned later that Dr. Maurice Druzin was originally from South Africa, where apartheid was still very much the law of the land. I would guess, from the way he greeted me, that his assumptions about black people had been molded in his home country. He was about five-foot-four and I towered over him by several inches. That probably didn't endear me to him, either.

Over lunch, he said that, at Cornell, even though I was a faculty member, I'd have to have a private practice, too, like any regular obstetrician.

"We're academics," I said, my expectations shaped by my years in medical school at Columbia and later, in the Navy. "We're perinatal specialists. We don't see private patients; we are consultants and do research."

"Not here," he replied. He told me that the salary I'd been offered in the letter from Cornell was only partly based on my duties as director of clinical services and a faculty member. I'd have to earn fully two-thirds of my pay by attracting private patients to the faculty practice that I was expected to establish within the hospital. In other words, two-thirds of what I believed was my salary was actually an advance against a share of the profits that my private practice was expected to bring to New York Hospital–Cornell Medical Center.

"If you don't carry your own weight, we're going to ask you to leave," he announced, matter-of-factly.

Just as I was reeling from the thought of having to establish a private practice—exactly what I'd taken several extra years of postdoctoral training to avoid doing—he added one last bit of information.

He could not make space for me in the department's offices, he said.

"We'll give you an office in the sub-basement, near the clinic."

Maybe they really had run out of space on the first floor, where the rest of the Obstetrics and Gynecology (OB-GYN) Department faculty had offices. Maybe the sub-basement really was the only other place they could put me. I couldn't help wondering though, if he would have made certain there was room above ground if I'd been a different color.

I tried to put that out of my mind and instead, focus on learning how to establish a private practice. I'd gone from medical school to a residency at Roosevelt Hospital to a post-doctoral fellowship and then into the military, always with academia rather than the business side of medicine in my sights. So now, I had to take a two-day crash course on how to set up a private practice to fill in the blanks of my knowledge about attracting paying patients. And I put on my best "show face" when I came to work.

About a week after my introduction to Cornell, the department chairman, Dr. William J. Ledger, called me into his office for a meeting. Although we'd greeted each other when we passed in the halls, we hadn't been formally introduced.

His office, of course, was on the first floor, but huge, and opulent by comparison to the office spaces used by other members of the OB-GYN faculty. His desk and bookcases were constructed of a rich, dark wood and had a sturdy, conservative look. Instead of the bland institutional seating typical in faculty doctors' offices, the chairman's guests enjoyed the comfort of well-padded wing chairs lushly upholstered in burgundy that coordinated with the thick rug that covered the office floor. His walls were decorated with the evidence of his substantial academic accomplishments. The effect of all this would have been more impressive if not for the clutter of paper that covered every surface, even spilling onto the chairs.

"Don't touch anything," he said, lightheartedly. "I know where everything is."

He pushed aside some files so I could sit in one of the wing chairs. Instead of sitting behind his desk, he took another wing chair across from me.

He seemed pleasant and friendly. I knew that Dr. Druzin was his fair-haired boy, but Dr. Ledger wasn't Dr. Druzin. I found myself relaxing in his presence as he asked how I was liking Cornell.

"It's like I died and went to heaven," I answered. Well, okay, maybe that wasn't quite my sentiment, but I wanted to make a good impression and show my enthusiasm.

He smiled and nodded. "What have you heard about me?" he asked, and I told him what I knew of his background as an expert in gynecological infections such as pelvic inflammatory disease. I'd also heard that he'd come to Cornell from California.

"What else have you heard? Good? Bad?" he asked. "Do you think I'm a racist?"

His words hit like a punch to the gut.

"I don't know. Are you?" was all I could think to say.

He didn't respond. He just kept smiling.

Smiling!

What did that mean?

I don't recall anything more of what was said in that meeting, nor could I tell you how long I was in his office before I left to get back to the sub-basement.

Throughout the day, those words echoed—*"Do you think I'm a racist?"*—and forced my memory back to a few months earlier, when Shearwood and I were preparing to leave the Navy. We had planned to buy a house near enough to New York City that we could commute but be in a quiet, kid-friendly, suburban neighborhood. So, we drove from Maryland to New Jersey every weekend to meet with our real estate agent and look at houses. On one of those weekends, the agent was showing us a lovely colonial in Franklin Lakes. Shearwood, Woody (Shearwood McClelland, III), Kimmie (Kimberly Itaska), and I were in the living room, trying to get a sense of what it would be like to call this place home. It was on a quiet street, had four bedrooms and a nice big backyard. I could imagine putting a swing set back there for Woody and Kimmie as they grew. I was wondering whether there were enough bathrooms when the owner called our agent into the kitchen.

"Get the niggers out of my house," she said, loud enough for us to hear. The children were too young to understand, and yet, the hurt I felt was, I think, more for them than for myself.

DO YOU THINK *that I'm a racist?*

I hadn't heard anything of the sort about the chairman, but the reception I'd gotten to date left me feeling as unwelcome at Cornell as I'd felt at that house in Franklin Lakes.

Whatever else happened, I was not about to let the chairman know how his words had stung. My daddy had drilled it into all us girls that it did you no good to let on when someone hurt you.

Everything I was and everything I had, right down to my wonderful husband, Shearwood, was mine thanks only to my parents' wise counsel.

I came home to the apartment we'd rented in Hackensack, New Jersey, that night, feeling very alone. Shearwood was in Ohio until January, completing a fellowship in hip replacement surgery. I put Woody and Kimmie to bed, then reached for the phone and called my parents' home.

My mother had died about five years earlier, in 1977. My father listened as I poured out my heart to him about how they put me in the sub-basement.

"Cookie," he called me by my childhood nickname, "They opened the door a crack. Now you have to prove to them who you are."

"Okay, but I have a feeling they don't like me here."

"So when have you ever been liked?" he answered. "What are you there for, a popularity contest? Are there patients to see that are sick?"

And I said yes, of course there were.

"Well, see the patients. You're not there for your colleagues. You're there to see the patients."

His words might not have offered the kind of comfort I'd been seeking, but I knew he was right. I was there to make a difference in my patients' lives, as much as I could, with my skills and my training. And if my colleagues didn't like me, so be it.

DADDY NEVER SUGAR-COATED anything. He never had, not even when we were tiny children. I remember him telling us why he wanted us to study hard so we could all grow up to be doctors.

"I love you better than I love life, but I'm not always gonna be around to look after you," he said. He was convinced that, without him, his five daughters would need to fend for themselves. Unlike lighter-skinned girls, he believed, we couldn't count on having our choice of husbands. It was the 1950s and, even among other African-Americans, dark skin like ours was considered unattractive. That's not the word Daddy used though. He called us ugly—not to hurt us but to impress upon us that that was the way the world viewed us and we had only ourselves and each other to count on.

"That's why you gotta be able to look after yourselves. And for that, you gotta be smart."

Daddy had only a tenth-grade education but what he lacked in formal schooling he more than made up for in his insights into human nature. He was a consummate social scientist. He and Mommy worked hard, too. Daddy had two full-time jobs and took on side jobs whenever he could. Mommy cleaned houses. She'd once dreamed of becoming a teacher but had to quit college for lack of money before she got her degree. Still, they both tried to make sure we children had whatever we needed.

When my oldest sister, Donna, was about seven years old, she begged my parents for a saxophone. A friend of Daddy's had one in his attic, which Daddy bought for twenty-five dollars, paying him five dollars a week. My next oldest sister, Jeanette, who accompanied Donna and my mother to Donna's saxophone lessons, soon convinced my parents to buy her a guitar. And then, it was my turn—I wanted to play the sax, too. So, Daddy took on more odd jobs to pay for our instruments and our lessons. Linda started drum lessons at age five.

Playing together as a band, we four oldest were good enough that Daddy decided we should play at a PTA meeting. By the time I was eight, we were playing local dances. Daddy got the idea that we could actually earn some money, at least enough to pay for our lessons and instruments. Rita, my youngest sister, started playing piano and Mommy learned the upright bass. Within a few years, we were on Ted Mack's *Original Amateur Hour* television show, had won the amateur contest six consecutive weeks at Harlem's legendary Apollo Theater, and then we went on to play weekend gigs at college dances. Daddy socked away the money we made to pay for our college tuition. He may have been just a blue-collar worker, a man who dug ditches during the day, drove a truck at night, and did odd jobs in between, but he had his dream of seeing his daughters grow up to become doctors. And three of us did become doctors, another was a court stenographer, and one was a science teacher.

I WAS MY FATHER'S daughter. I was living his dream—and on the path to realizing my own. I wasn't going to let small, closed minds slam the door against me. I planned to rise as high in my profession as my skills and hard work would allow. I was a black woman but that wasn't going to stop me from striving to be the best doctor it was possible to be.

I'd pass along my parents' wisdom to my own children so that they, too, could beat the odds and succeed. I'd already decided (just as my father had, for me and my sisters, when I was still a little girl), that they could shoot for any career they wanted ... as long as it came with an MD after their names.

THE FOLLOWING MORNING, WITH Daddy's words crowding those of the chairman out of my thoughts, I got back to work.

But I was again struck by how dismal the sub-basement was. There was nothing here to suggest the joy a woman feels at becoming a mother. The clinic hadn't been updated since the 1930s, and it showed. The examining rooms with their battleship-gray walls and cold, ancient metal exam tables and stirrups were bad enough. The worst of it was how the rooms were laid out. The entrance to each exam room was through a curtain; there were no doors. A stool was set up for the doctor in front of each table, and the patient would be lying there waiting, her feet in the stirrups. Open the curtain, and you're facing the woman's exposed perineum, vagina and all.

I realized that this made it convenient for a doctor to move quickly from patient to patient, sit down, do a Pap smear, move on to the next, and so on. The setup, however, showed no respect for a patient's sense of modesty.

"Luradine," I said to the nurse, "what if someone just wants to peek over the curtain and ask a question?"

Luradine Timberlake, one of the head clinic nurses, acknowledged that the patients' feelings weren't considered in deciding how the tables were arranged but then, the clinic was for poor people. The layout wasn't up to the patients and it wasn't up to her. No doctor had ever thought to change it.

"Well, we're changing it now," I said.

Luradine and I moved the examination tables clockwise ninety degrees so that, when you opened the curtain, you'd see a woman's modestly draped side, not her exposed vagina. Then we moved the stools next to the wall, so when a doctor entered, everything was still ready and accessible, but, if someone should inadvertently open the curtain—no harm done.

The Sub-Basement and the Glass Ceiling

WITH THAT SMALL BUT important change completed, I started to look for other ways the clinic could be improved.

I asked the chairman for better equipment but he said no. That's all we have, and we don't have a budget for anything more.

He seemed genuinely perplexed at why I even thought it was an issue.

"It's been there for forty-five years. Why do you want to change it?"

How do you explain to a man, even a male obstetrician, that a woman's sensitivities are different from his, that no woman wants to be in a dark, dank, dungeon-like sub-basement?

I might as well have tried to convince a turnip for all the progress I made.

His answer, whenever I brought up the topic, was that we didn't have the budget for new chairs, for new exam tables, not even for new reading material in the waiting room.

This was the New York Hospital Lying-In, said the chairman. This is the way it's always been and that's the way it would stay.

Strangely enough, though, the hospital found the money to renovate the part of the sub-basement where they wanted me to set up my new practice to see *paying* patients. For that, there was a budget to buy new exam tables, new everything.

The residents, not the faculty, had the primary responsibility for seeing patients in the free clinic. As a faculty member, training the residents, I would examine the patients along with them. Or, when a patient couldn't afford to come to see me in the private practice the hospital required me to have, I would see her in the clinic. The glumness of the place never ceased to bother me.

So, I tried to talk to the chairman again. I again got the "we don't have the budget" speech.

"All right then," I said. "May I at least have some paint?"

"I don't know. How much is the paint?"

I told him I didn't know either. "But it can't be that much."

"All right. Paint the clinic. But that's all we can do."

"I would like to paint it yellow."

"Fine," he answered. He probably would have agreed to purple polka dots if it meant getting me out of his hair.

And boy, when it was done was it ever bright. It was all lemony sunshine, about as different from institutional gray as it was possible to get. Still, even with a cheery color, blank, naked walls leave a lot to be desired.

We needed something to decorate the clinic. I knew I wouldn't get anything more from the chairman. His mantra played in my head like a needle stuck in a record's groove: no budget, no budget, no budget.

WHILE ON ONE OF the upper floors of the New York Hospital, I noticed the bright, happy paintings on the walls.

"Who put up those paintings of flowers?" I asked a nurse.

"Oh, those? They're from the volunteers in the Ladies Auxiliary."

I got the phone number for the Ladies Auxiliary, and called right away.

"Would you mind coming down to the sub-basement and looking at our walls?" I asked. "It's only in the clinic, but ..."

No problem at all, said the woman on the other end of the line. They'd be delighted.

The next thing I knew, these very nice women from the Ladies Auxiliary were giving the sub-basement clinic's walls their full attention, pondering decorating decisions with as much care as I'd expect them to give the chairman's office.

"Well, this should go here, don't you think?" said one woman, holding up a painting of a mother and child.

Another held up a lovely still life against the bright yellow wall in the waiting room and asked for opinions.

A Madonna and child portrait here, a still life with flowers there, and that ugly old sub-basement started looking beautiful.

But they didn't stop at paintings. The Ladies Auxiliary came in with armloads of treasures. Before they were done, we had magazines on the tables in the waiting room and better chairs. You could see the difference, not just on the walls and in the furniture but also in the faces of the patients. When I first got the okay for the bright yellow paint, Dr. Wilma Gladstone, an attending physician in endocrinology, was somewhat taken aback.

"My god, Yvonne, why did you have to paint it this shocking yellow?"

After the paintings went up and the new chairs came in, though, she loved the transformation. It looked even better than I'd imagined.

Of course, the chairman didn't care one way or the other and I don't think he was any happier to have me in his department than on the first day we met. Neither, I imagine, was Dr. Druzin.

something to prove

It didn't trouble me so much any more. The patients appreciated what I was doing. They understood that I was on their side. And I sensed that they were on mine.

That, I realized, thinking back to Daddy's words of advice, was all that really mattered.

chapter two

There's a Call for Dr. Thornton

"I wanted [my daughters] to be strong... They would
never be at the mercy of anyone, like I was."
                                    —DONALD THORNTON

BEING A WOMAN GAVE me a different perspective than the male physicians had, and it showed—not just in the changes I made in the clinic but in the way I ran my new private practice at Cornell. There were some things that no man, however sensitive, could completely understand. And the less sensitive ones probably didn't want to understand.

Because I could empathize with my patients about the many little indignities, and the discomfort, of gynecological examinations, I set about making their visits as pleasant as possible.

When I had my own annual gynecologic exam, for instance, I hated the chill of that cold metal clamp my OB-GYN used. Recognizing that other women probably felt the same, I always set my metal speculum in warm water before I used it in an examination.

I looked at those awful hospital gowns and wondered, what sort of sadist designed the things? Whether they opened in the front or back, a woman always felt all exposed. I had pretty new blue gowns made that were more like ponchos, with an opening in the middle to go over the patient's head. They covered everything that should be covered, which my patients really appreciated.

Every time a woman thanked me for thinking as only another woman could, I got psyched and looked for more ways to improve the experience. When I saw an ad for mink stirrup covers in an OB-GYN newsletter, I knew they'd be a hit and ordered some right away.

Pretty soon, my fur-covered stirrups were the talk of the office. Not only were they comfy, but they definitely lightened the mood.

I wanted my patients to have something unique to look at instead of the blank, ugly ceiling during exams. So, I went to an arts and crafts store, got a couple of mobile kits, and attached the finished mobiles above my examination tables. Now, while I was examining my patient, she could examine the butterflies, flowers, and birds dancing above her head.

Word spread about all those thoughtful little touches and by the beginning of 1983, much to my own surprise, I had a thriving private practice in my sub-basement office at New York Hospital–Cornell Medical Center.

I wasn't following the rules for successful doctors in other ways, either. Most physicians in private practice understood that if they hustled patients out the door when their appointment times were up, they could squeeze in more appointments. My academic base salary was a pittance. The bulk of my compensation came from my faculty practice, and the chairman made clear that he expected his doctors to see as many patients as possible during their office hours and operating room schedule. But I treated my patients the way I wanted to be treated, spent the time that was necessary, and the clock be damned.

I admit that that meant my patients couldn't exactly set their watches by my appointment calendar but when you're an OB-GYN, something unexpected always seems to come up.

For example, one day, after I'd finished an examination and was about to leave the exam room, I could see by my patient's expression that she had something else on her mind. So I waited a beat before saying good-bye. She hesitated and then blurted it out.

"Dr. Thornton, my husband's been unfaithful."

Well, I couldn't just leave her there and say, "That's a shame. Have a nice day." So I took her hand, sat her back down, and asked why she suspected that, taking care to be neutral and professional. After she explained how she'd found out, I told her we should test for STDs and herpes, which meant getting her back in the stirrups. That took another few minutes. When I'd done what I could for her in my professional capacity, I could see she still needed more from me. She needed a shoulder. So I hugged her and she cried and I listened as she poured out the hurt and confusion she felt. Then I sat with her as she composed herself enough to leave the exam room and face the world.

With my focus on whomever I was examining, I had no way of knowing what was happening in my waiting room. My receptionist clued me in, though, after a new patient loudly complained that she'd been waiting long past her appointment time.

The other ladies, all established patients, gently took the new patient in hand and told her to sit down, relax, and enjoy some candy from the large glass bowl I filled each morning. "Because when Dr. Thornton gets to you," my receptionist later told me one of them said, "it's like nobody else exists."

That woman decided to stay, appreciative that I sat, listened, and took care of her. But plenty of others switched to doctors who could be counted on to get them in and out on schedule. Even so, my appointment book was filled as more of my patients sent their friends, daughters, sisters, and mothers to see me.

DESPITE THE PRIVATE PRACTICE that Cornell insisted I have, I was still primarily an academic—an attending physician who trained and supervised OB-GYN residents and maternal-fetal medicine fellows. Other than rotating teaching duties from week to week with Dr. Druzin, he and I operated separately from each other. I could almost forget the chilly greeting he gave me when I first arrived. I shouldn't have been surprised when he refused to cover for me during the vacation I'd planned for June. With no other maternal-fetal medicine specialist on staff to take care of my patients, it meant no vacation for me that year. Fine. I'd cope. There were other situations, however, where I had to draw the line.

There's a Call for Dr. Thornton

On rounds one day with residents, we had a mother with Rh-negative blood who had given birth to an Rh-positive baby. Before some relatively recent medical advances, an Rh-negative mother's immune system would often mistakenly react to an Rh-positive fetus as if it were an invading organism. And the result would be a "blue baby"—one whose blood cells are attacked by antibodies in the mother's womb. But thanks to RhoGAM, blue babies are rare today and an Rh-negative mother can safely carry her Rh-positive child to term. RhoGAM is a blood product that already has antibodies in it and it keeps the mother's body from forming her own. And without the mother's antibodies trying to attack the baby's red blood cells, the baby will be safe. So, we give the mother RhoGAM at 28 weeks into the pregnancy and again, within three days of delivery to prevent her body from reacting to the cells of any subsequent Rh-positive child.

In this case, though, we had a mother who had delivered more than three days earlier and hadn't gotten her RhoGAM injection. I told the residents to check the patient's blood to see if she was developing antibodies and if not, give her an injection of RhoGAM. I'd trained at Columbia where RhoGAM was developed, so I knew that although it hadn't been tested for effectiveness more than seventy-two hours after delivery, it also hadn't been shown to be ineffective. We couldn't rule out the possibility that giving it now could later save a baby's life.

The following week, the residents were on rounds with Dr. Druzin as the attending. And then, following him in rotation, it was once more my turn to teach them.

something to prove

As we again discussed management of an Rh-negative mother with an Rh-positive baby, one of the residents told me that Dr. Druzin had dismissed what I'd taught them. According to this resident, Druzin claimed that RhoGAM should be given within seventy-two hours and that "Yvonne doesn't know what she's talking about."

It was all I could do to make it through rounds before I marched over to the chairman's office.

I told Dr. Ledger what my resident said and reminded Dr. Ledger that no attending physician should ever tear down another's credibility, especially in front of the residents.

"If Dr. Druzin has a difference of opinion with me, he can come to me and discuss it," I said. "I won't put up with him undermining me with my residents."

Ledger listened without comment until I'd finished.

"You know, Morrie's had some problems," he said.

I didn't care what "Morrie's" personal problems were, I said. I expected Dr. Morrie Druzin to treat me as a peer.

"I'll take care of Morrie," Dr. Ledger assured me.

And—in that instance, at least—he did.

That was the first and last time I heard of Dr. Druzin denigrating me in front of the residents. I had no illusions; I knew Dr. Druzin's attitude toward me wouldn't change. I suspected that I would never overcome what he viewed as the deficits he associated with my race and gender. But I'd won this battle.

My training, my knowledge, and my Board certification were equal to Dr. Druzin's, and so were my accomplishments. He'd just have to learn to accept that, even if he couldn't accept me.

There's a Call for Dr. Thornton

I DIDN'T HAVE ANY illusions about the chairman's attitude toward me, either. Stopping Druzin from tearing down a fellow attending physician in front of the residents was one thing. But seeing me as a member of the club wasn't in the cards. I could sense Dr. Ledger's coolness toward me even when he was outwardly supporting me.

I reminded myself of my father's advice—what my colleagues thought didn't matter—but I wasn't made of stone. Food had been my comfort since I was a little girl and I needed a lot of comfort right then. That night, I went to bed early with a pint of strawberry Häagen-Dazs ice cream.

But some time later, when it came time to apply to a more formal "club," where admission was based on professional achievement and knowledge, it took all my strength to keep my composure.

The New York Obstetrical Society is a very prestigious obstetrical society located in New York City and one of the oldest OB-GYN organizations in the country—second only to The Philadelphia Obstetrical Society. During my residency at Roosevelt Hospital in the 1970s, one of my mentors, Dr. Thomas F. Dillon, who eventually became president of the society, had taken us residents to its meetings as his guests. The society met at the elite Yale Club on Vanderbilt Avenue. Here, in a room that was the epitome of sophistication and elegance, members and their guests assembled. Decked out in tuxedoes and clustered in small groups, almost all the members were men, and they were among the most prominent, renowned physicians in our specialty. The society adhered to unwavering tradition, right down to what was served as the first course for dinner: always black bean soup.

But its most important tradition was that it was extremely selective. A faculty OB-GYN at any academic medical center in New York would have given his right arm to become a member.

Back then, for me, membership seemed a distant dream, but Dr. Dillon assured me that if I worked hard, published papers, and achieved what he believed I was capable of, someday I'd be accepted.

Now that I was an OB-GYN on faculty at Cornell, I was expected to apply to the society. Drs. Druzin and Ledger belonged, and both were lobbying hard for Ledger's right-hand man, Dr. Alan Berkeley, to be accepted too. Because I was in his department, Ledger also proposed me for membership. As I would discover, that didn't mean he was lending full support to my application.

The Obstetrical Society membership committee convened in the medical library of the New York Hospital OB-GYN Department to evaluate new candidates from Cornell. It was a sumptuous room, with a beamed ceiling, rich mahogany paneling, and high, arched bay windows overlooking the East River. Barrister bookcases filled with books and bound journals lined the walls from floor to ceiling. Thick carpeting absorbed the sounds of our footsteps as we entered. I relaxed somewhat when I saw that another of my mentors from my days at Roosevelt, Dr. Ernst Bartsich, was on the membership committee.

The New York Obstetrical Society panel sat behind a big mahogany conference table and those of us from Cornell sat before them in chairs—me on the right, Dr. Ledger in the center, and Dr. Berkeley to his left.

There's a Call for Dr. Thornton

When one of the committee members asked Dr. Ledger why he believed the two candidates he'd proposed were accomplished enough to become members, the chairman went on at great length about how Alan Berkeley was his right-hand man, how Berkeley was indispensable, how Ledger couldn't function without Berkeley, and that even though Berkeley did not have his Board certification in either reproductive endocrinology or gynecologic oncology, he'd done important work in infertility as a fellow for one year at Yale. Ledger continued to praise Berkeley for several minutes straight.

"He is the director of our residency program. I could not do anything in OB-GYN without Alan Berkeley," the chairman ended emphatically. "I rely on him."

When he'd finished, a panel member asked him what he thought of Dr. Thornton.

"Oh, she's okay," said Ledger.

She's okay? That's it?

He never said another word.

Knock me over with a feather. He didn't want me to get in.

He had to propose my name; I was in his department. But he wasn't going to do more than the absolute minimum. If I could have crawled out of the library with no one noticing, I would have. Instead, I sat there, smiling as if everything was fine and the chairman had said no more or less than what I expected. I looked up at Dr. Bartsich and wondered what he was thinking, but his expression gave away nothing.

If the recommendation of the person proposing my membership was the determining factor, my chances had just been shattered.

33

something to prove

ALL THE ATTENDING PHYSICIANS wanted Fridays off so they could enjoy a long weekend. The ones with seniority got their wish. As the new kid on the Cornell block, for me, Fridays were work days.

The Friday before Lincoln's birthday, February 11, 1983, was a holiday for Harlem Hospital, where Shearwood was Assistant Director of Orthopedics. The nursery school Woody and Kimmie attended was closed as well. But the New York Hospital– Cornell Medical Center clinics were open so, while Shearwood stayed home with the kids, I trudged over the George Washington Bridge and down to New York Hospital in my big blue four-door Chevrolet Monte Carlo.

The sky was a dismal gray when I left home. The weather report threatened a powerful nor'easter but there were no storm clouds yet. I wasn't too worried. I'd long since figured out that if I wanted an accurate prediction of whether it would snow, I could just as easily flip a coin as rely on the weatherman.

My schedule was packed and, as usual, appointments were running a bit long. It always seemed that I was on time until that last moment, as I was about to end my appointment with one patient to turn my attention to the next. I'd be joking with a woman as I prepared to leave when she'd bring up just one more question. Today, it was, "Dr. Thornton, you just made me laugh and I realized I forgot to tell you. When I laugh, I pee a little." So I took a few more minutes with her to order a urine culture and perform some other tests before moving on to the next patient.

Katie Sontag was waiting in exam room #2. She was an attractive woman in her mid-thirties with a pixie-like haircut and perky personality to match. Katie said she'd had some spotting and pain and had missed two periods. Her temperature was normal and she had no other signs of an infection. Although her urine pregnancy tests had come back negative, my mantra, under the circumstances, is "Pregnant until proven otherwise." I suspected that a fertilized egg might have lodged in one of her fallopian tubes. If such an "ectopic" pregnancy were allowed to keep growing, the fallopian tube could burst, endangering Katie's life.

On her abdominal exam, she winced every time I touched her right side. During my internal exam, I discovered a bulge in her vagina. When I probed the bulge with a needle, my syringe filled with blood, meaning she was bleeding internally.

It was a good thing she hadn't waited to come in, I told her, because we'd have to do immediate surgery.

We got her right into an operating room and, as expected, Katie had a ruptured ectopic pregnancy. I found the fallopian tube on her right side so damaged that I couldn't save it. But, she still had another healthy fallopian tube. She'd still have a chance to get pregnant in the future.

I joined her in the recovery room when she awoke to make sure she was all right, and to assure her that I'd check in over the weekend. It was the first time since getting to the hospital that I'd looked out a window. The sub-basement was below ground level and the OR didn't have any.

I wasn't prepared for what we saw through the glass. I never knew snowflakes could be that fat or tumble down so heavily. While I'd been performing a delicate surgery, oblivious to everything but my patient, the blizzard to end all blizzards had whipped into New York.

something to prove

I CALLED HOME BEFORE leaving the hospital and Shear-wood offered to come get me but I'd told him no. Stay with the kids, I said. I'll be home as soon as possible.

I pulled out of the hospital's underground garage and into the city streets. Traffic had simply stopped. If not for the exhaust fumes rising from the cars all around me and the swishing of wipers, this major midtown Manhattan thoroughfare could have been mistaken for a miles-long, snow-covered parking lot.

We crawled a few inches, then braked and waited, making a snail's progress toward the east and the FDR Drive. My Monte Carlo was a newer car and I'd recently replaced the windshield wipers but it was as if the gods were throwing snowballs down at us from the skies. The snow packed itself on either side of the blades. I strained to see where I was going. At about two miles per hour, I wasn't going far.

AT 8:00 THAT NIGHT I was nearing the entrance ramp to the George Washington Bridge, a distance that I normally traveled in just under twenty minutes. I'd left the hospital at 2:00 in the afternoon. All along the way, stalled cars littered the breakdown lanes and fishtailing vehicles presented roadblocks to navigate around. But I was at most, a few miles from home.

Shearwood had paged me about a half-dozen times and I felt bad that I had no way of calling to let him know I was all right.

A few car lengths ahead of me, someone drove up the ramp, got about two-thirds of the way, and skidded backwards. The next vehicle tried to pull around, got to about the same point, and—nothing. His tires spun, his engine squealed, and the car slid in reverse. The ramp to the George Washington Bridge was like a skating rink for cars. Some glided sideways or did half-turns and pirouettes. Others wiggled and wobbled in place. But none advanced past the two-thirds mark on the ramp.

I looked behind me, not knowing what to do. For as far as I could see, through the snow-filled air, cars and trucks were backed up waiting to get onto the bridge. Nothing was moving.

From one of the cars ahead of me, a driver's door opened and a husky man, huddled in his coat, probably in his mid-forties, got out and headed back toward the line of waiting vehicles. He had a decidedly military bearing and he banged on windows as he walked.

"C'mon," he yelled. "We've got to help each other or none of us is getting out of here."

I stepped out of the Monte Carlo to help and my black mid-heel pumps instantly filled with slush and snow. The wind was brutal. Bundling my collar around my neck, I joined several other drivers at the back of the first car on the ramp and heaved with all my might. We pushed it uphill about ten feet before the car gained traction on the road and, after a brief fishtail, made it over the hitch.

My toes were threatening to go numb as I moved on to the next car and with the other drivers, pushed again. Four feet, five feet, uphill, fighting against gravity and the slick, icy slush, this group of tired strangers somehow found the strength to keep the pressure on until the car's engine took over. Away it went, its exhaust blasting our faces.

It was my turn next and I said a silent prayer as I got back in my car and steered while the citizen brigade helped push me over the hump. At first, the tires protested and then, as if nothing had impeded the way, the Chevy got purchase on the road and sailed up the ramp.

As I drove the length of the bridge, I heard the wind gusts whistling across the water and felt them push against the car. Snow on the roadway got whipped up into little whirlwinds, mixing with the bucketsful tossed down from above.

Slowly, cautiously, I made my way to the Teaneck exit. I barely recognized the landscape when I got off the bridge. Abandoned cars and trucks littered the roads, and the blizzard obscured landmarks and signs.

AT 2:00 A.M., TWELVE HOURS since I'd left the hospital, I was finally driving on my own street. I could see my house ahead and steered toward it only to run out of gas just a few doors away. No problem, I thought … until I tried to open my door. A snowbank blocked me in.

What else could go wrong?

Somehow, I pushed the door open enough to squeeze out, trekked the several yards to my house, and literally fell into Shearwood's arms, frozen, exhausted, and sobbing, as he guided me into the house.

Home had never looked so good before.

SHEARWOOD ISN'T A TALKATIVE guy. Pick any strong, silent type man you know and I'll guarantee you, next to my Shearwood, he'll look like a chatterbox. So, Shearwood didn't go on and on about how worried he'd been, waiting at home, while I made my way through the blizzard that dumped more than seventeen inches on the city and that the newscasters were calling the "megapolitan" snowstorm. Instead, he just held me and comforted me as I babbled about my ordeal. And the following morning, he showed his concern by doing something he'd never done before: he brought me breakfast in bed.

Granted, Shearwood is not much of a chef. He rarely goes near the stove to do more than boil water. So the eggs were undercooked and the toast was burnt, but I couldn't have asked for a lovelier way to wake up than with this sweet if slightly inept gesture from my big, strong, wonderful husband.

I was sipping orange juice and poking at my half-cooked eggs when the phone rang. It was my uncle on the line, my father's brother. If I'd thought that last night's twelve-hour odyssey through a blizzard was the worst that could happen to me, I was wrong.

My father had had a stroke, Uncle Milford said. He was in the hospital.

I ASKED OUR HOUSEKEEPER, to watch Woody and Kimmie so that Shearwood and I could rush to Red Bank, New Jersey to be with Daddy.

Unconscious and unresponsive—that's how his doctors described him. No one could say for sure that he would ever come out of it.

I'm a doctor. I know what it means to be in a coma. And yet, it seemed impossible that this vibrant, determined man who, at times, seemed a force of nature could lie there in such still-ness, unable to respond to my pleas for him to open his eyes.

One after another, my sisters arrived—Donna, Rita, Linda,

and our foster sister, Betty. Only Jeanette, the second oldest of the five Thornton sisters, didn't make it to Daddy's bedside. She and her husband, Emile Powe, a postdoctoral fellow in gastroenterology she'd met when she was an intern, were in Nigeria. As a condition of a grant Emile had received, he'd agreed to serve for a year in the public health service in Africa.

Daddy's neurologist prepared us for the worst. There was massive brain damage from the stroke. He appeared to be slipping away.

Shearwood took me home but we returned to Daddy's bedside the next day. Nothing had changed. Except now, when I looked at Daddy, I thought I could see a slight smile on his face. And I wondered what he felt at that moment. Was his an expectant smile? Was he hoping to see my mother again? Daddy had never been much of a churchgoer. I figured he believed in the Almighty, but I didn't quite know. What I'd mostly seen of his faith through my life was his belief in his family.

I thought back to six years earlier when Mommy died, and how all the divorced and widowed ladies in the neighborhood had come around, bringing cakes and casseroles, trying to coax Daddy into a new romance.

One woman in particular seemed set on catching Daddy's eye. Her name was Catherine and she was a few years older than he was but you'd never know it to look at her. She had a body to die for. Raquel Welch had nothing on this lady, never mind that Catherine was past sixty.

But Daddy wasn't impressed. He missed his Tass, Itasker Frances Thornton, his wife of thirty-four years.

The ladies didn't give up the quest easily though. Daddy

had bought himself a new white Mercedes convertible the year before, the only non-American car he ever owned, and he wanted a car phone to go with it. They were the newest thing but difficult to get unless you had Hollywood connections or you knew someone at the phone company.

Catherine worked for the phone company and arranged to have a car phone installed in Daddy's shiny new Mercedes convertible. I think she would have done just about anything for him, and we tried to persuade him to give her or one of the other ladies a chance. No luck. He had loved only one woman in his life, he said. His Tass; my mom. There would never be room in his heart for another, never mind the temptations of a gorgeous body or high-tech gadgets.

I'd like to believe he was reunited with his Tass when, on February 15, 1983, he died without ever regaining consciousness.

DADDY HAD ALWAYS SAID that every one of his daughters could do anything that a man could do. So, as we had when my mother died, my sisters and I acted as his pallbearers carrying that heavy coffin up the snow-covered hill to his final resting place.

I watched his casket lowered into the ground, but for me, he could never really be gone, not as long as I still lived. Even though I could no longer pick up the phone and call, I could still hear his voice guiding me when I wasn't sure what to do. His belief in his daughters' abilities, his support, and his love had helped make me the woman I was. I carried him in my heart—and I knew I would always find him there when I needed him.

something to prove

I THINK I WAS in a fog those weeks after Daddy died. But I had my own responsibilities and kept going—getting the kids ready for nursery school, making more little changes to spruce up the clinic, and answering those urgent calls telling me it was time to rush to the hospital to deliver new life into the world. Babies are an amazing and beautiful affirmation that no matter what we face, life goes on, with all its possibility and wonder and hope.

I couldn't ask for a better life for myself than this. And I wouldn't be living it if not for Daddy's faith in me, and in all my sisters.

Strangely enough, it hadn't started out as faith. I hadn't known this until Mommy told me when I was in the second grade, but when Daddy first talked about our becoming doctors, it was just a way to deflect the ribbing from his brothers and his fellow laborers for having nothing but girls in his family. The men Daddy worked with called his wife and five daughters Donald's "six splits." With not a single son, they chided, he'd never have anyone to carry on his name. So, Donald Thornton razzed them right back, telling them, "You won't be laughing when my little girls grow up to be doctors and everyone will be callin' them 'Dr. Thornton.'"

The other laborers thought this was a hoot and needled him even more. But he insisted we'd all grow up to wear "scripperscraps" around our necks—his word for stethoscopes—as he defended what seemed at the time an outrageous boast. Maybe it was, but somewhere along the way, Daddy figured out that this really could be his children's path to the security and respect that always had eluded him. Outrageous or not, he became committed to the idea. And so did my mother.

When I look back, I see that my parents planned for our future success with such foresight, determination, and wisdom that a Nobel Laureate would have had trouble besting them.

Mommy and Daddy knew better than anyone that being black, and being female besides, their children were born with a double handicap. If we girls were going to get any breaks, my parents knew it would be the breaks we made for ourselves. We had to pull so far ahead that nothing and no one could hold us back. Most parents would be thrilled if their little girls came home with report cards that had nothing but straight As. Not my Daddy. Not as long as an A-plus was possible. My sister Jeanette always complained he was overly strict, and there's no denying that he was. But where would we all be now if he hadn't been?

MANY YEARS AFTER MY mother had died, we took Daddy out for his birthday at Shadowbrook, one of those hoity-toity restaurants that we couldn't afford when we were kids. It was all very elegant, with waiters in tuxedoes and drinks served in crystal. It also didn't hurt that it had some of the best prime rib in New Jersey. Daddy was always a meat-and-potatoes kind of guy.

My sister Linda, the second youngest, had come to town from Fort Meade, Maryland, where she was stationed. She was in the dental corps and an Army major. My sister Jeanette had just finished medical school after originally getting her degree in psychology. Daddy had always expected her to be the first Dr. Thornton, the first to have a "scripperscrap" around her neck, but she'd rebelled and gone her own way. So he must have been thrilled when she finally got her medical degree, even if it came later than he'd hoped.

It had been a while but we were all there, just him and his girls again, the way Daddy liked it, no kids, no husbands.

The waiters had already brought the salad and I had arranged a little surprise before the main course.

The maître d' came to the table and announced, "There's a call for Dr. Thornton."

Some curious diners turned to see who was Dr. Thornton. Jeanette, Linda and I rose from our chairs and as we stood up, the look on my father's face could have lit up the entire Eastern seaboard.

There wasn't really any call. I'd taken the maître d' aside earlier and asked him to page "Dr. Thornton" during dinner because I wanted to see the wonderment on my father's face when three of his daughters stood up to answer. Each of us was "Dr. Thornton." We were the living proof that Daddy had done what he set out to do.

Daddy marveled at us standing there, as if he couldn't quite believe he'd actually managed to achieve this impossible dream. All his work, all his sacrifice had paid off.

He was too tough to cry, especially in front of us girls, but if there were ever a time when he came close, that was it. And I knew it was the best birthday present we could have given him.

Learning to Play the Game

I N THE SPRING OF 1983, not too long after Daddy died, Dr. Ledger summoned me to his office. Ten major academic hospitals were going to be involved in FDA trials of a type of prenatal testing that could be done in early pregnancy, called chorionic villus sampling—CVS for short.

"It's a new technique that is probably a flash in the pan," explained the chairman. Amniocentesis accomplished the same result as CVS and was the established procedure for prenatal genetic testing. Still, the chairman didn't want our medical center to be left behind. Someone at Cornell should know how to do it. He told me to go up to Mount Sinai Medical Center, one of the ten hospitals involved in the trials, and ask Dr. Bob Desnick, the lead investigator, to teach me the technique.

Like amniocentesis, CVS testing gives parents-to-be an early warning on genetic diseases such as Tay-Sachs and Down syndrome. Unlike amnio, CVS testing does not have to wait until the mother is at least sixteen weeks pregnant. CVS can be done as early as ten weeks into a pregnancy, which gives pregnant women that much extra time to weigh their options if genetic problems are discovered. CVS, like amniocentesis, also tells parents whether their baby is a boy or girl.

The test had originated in Denmark in 1968 and was further developed in China, where a one-child policy made the test popular among parents who were determined that the one child they were allowed to bring to term would be a boy.

Problems arose though, when the test became popular in the United States in 1982. A number of doctors who hadn't received proper training with the device used in the procedure started performing CVS in their offices. Reports filtered back to the FDA of unintended miscarriages, ruptured membranes, perforated uteruses, infections, and emergency hysterectomies.

That's when the FDA put the brakes on and said nobody could do CVS testing until it was studied and proven to be safe.

I knew next to nothing about CVS at the time, but when Dr. Ledger said, "Why don't you learn it, Yvonne?" I ran with it.

I rarely had occasion to visit other hospitals and it had been years since I'd been to Mount Sinai. On the Upper East Side, skirting the border of Central Park, Mount Sinai, like many major academic medical centers, sprawled across several city blocks. Its buildings were a hodgepodge of uninspired concrete architecture from the early 20th century, but as an academic facility it was first-rate. When I first graduated from medical school, I'd applied to the hospital's residency program. The interviewer who had been impressed with my grades, was less impressed when he saw me in the flesh.

"We don't accept black people," he said. "I don't think you would fit in."

I was too stunned at the time to say much more than, "Thank you for telling me."

That episode still stung, but I reminded myself that that was a different person and a whole different situation. I'd come a long way since then, despite bias.

Dr. Desnick, a dark-haired man of about forty, greeted me pleasantly enough. If his demeanor was welcoming, his message, when I asked him if he would train me in CVS, was quite the opposite.

"Now, why would I want to do that?" he said. "That would be the same as taking a potato off my plate." He explained that he thought if I learned the procedure, patients who might have gone to Mount Sinai would, instead, go to Cornell.

I should stop here and explain that an important tradition of academic medicine is the sharing of information and techniques. Everything I know about medicine, I learned from other academics who freely shared their knowledge. And in turn, I shared that knowledge with my residents and fellows, and any other physician who asked. The free and open exchange of medical knowledge and experience leaves all of us better off, doctors as well as patients. More important: without that tradition the academic system would collapse.

So Dr. Desnick's attitude surprised me.

I tried to persuade him that his "potato" was secure. Cornell is in midtown, I reminded him. Mount Sinai is on 100th Street. We served different populations.

He wouldn't hear of it. As far as he was concerned, if a woman in New York City wanted CVS, she'd need to go to Mount Sinai. Maybe he couldn't prevent another medical center from offering the technique, but he certainly wasn't going to help. This was his turf and I was a trespasser.

I reported back to Dr. Ledger that Desnick had refused me. The chairman said not to worry and invited Dr. Ron Wapner of Philadelphia's Thomas Jefferson University Hospital, another of the ten academic medical centers approved to conduct the FDA trials, to come to Cornell to give us a presentation on the technique.

Dr. Wapner was a delight, as generous with his knowledge as Desnick was stingy. About my age, he had a mop of unruly brown curls, an infectious smile, and the optimistic attitude of a football cheerleader. I liked him on sight.

Because of the FDA restrictions, Dr. Wapner couldn't demonstrate the procedure on a patient, but he showed us a video of how CVS was done.

With a combination of filmed and animated segments, the video showed an OB-GYN inserting a flexible catheter, no wider than a strand of spaghetti, through the vagina and just beyond the cervix (the mouth of the uterus) into the womb, navigating the catheter to avoid the fetus and the amniotic sac. Ultrasound, done by a specially trained sonographer, guided the OB-GYN's hand during the process. Inside the catheter was an even tinier flexible metal rod that looked almost like the dipstick you would use to check the oil in your car. When the ultrasound showed that the catheter had reached the placenta, the OB-GYN removed the dipstick-like rod, applied a fluid-filled syringe to the catheter, pulled back on the plunger to create a vacuum, and collected the cells from the growing placenta. These cells were then sent to a lab for analysis.

The video demonstration was great, but it was no substitute for hands-on training in the procedure. I thought of one of Daddy's favorite sayings. *If the front door is locked, go around and try the back door.*

"What if I bring a team to Philadelphia?" I asked. "Would you train us?"

"Absolutely," said Dr. Wapner.

A few weeks later, I had my team. Ed Quest was a lanky guy, about six-foot-three, with a lush moustache and dark hair. He was soft-spoken and gentle, and my patients loved him. Most important for this technique, though, he was a brilliant sonographer and had the steady hand necessary to locate that catheter within the womb. I chose Dr. Lita Alonso as the team's pathologist. Meticulous as they come, this tall, serious South American whiz seemed the perfect choice for a specialized task.

The three of us piled into my Monte Carlo, and off we drove to Philly.

I CAME BACK FROM my training with Dr. Wapner at Jefferson as psyched as I've ever been about a procedure. I could see that CVS offered tremendous benefits over amniocentesis. For one thing, it was simply more comfortable for the mother than having a big needle plunged into her belly. Most important, though, was the timing factor. I'd seen how difficult it was for expectant parents who'd invested hope and anticipation in a pregnancy to face the news that their child could have a serious genetic disorder such as Tay-Sachs disease, which can mean a brief and painful life. I believed that the decision not to carry such a child to term might be less emotionally wrenching if a woman learned the news in the first trimester rather than after four or five months of pregnancy.

I told Dr. Ledger I wanted to apply to join the FDA trials of the CVS device. The chairman warmed to the idea immediately but wanted to make one important change. He wanted Dr. Fritz Fuchs to apply to the FDA.

"He'll get that approval for you," said Ledger. "He has connections in the FDA."

Dr. Fuchs, a world renowned OB-GYN at Cornell, had pioneered amniocentesis. I knew if he helped with the FDA application process, even if I did most of the work, I would be relegated to an afterthought and he would get the credit. I don't know why but I was sure I could do this myself, without any outside help. So I told Dr. Ledger thanks, but I could handle it.

I WORKED LIKE CRAZY to get the chorionic villus sampling paperwork together for FDA approval, and as Ledger had warned me, it was a nightmare. There was no denying that. But I was plowing through it.

Back in the clinic, I had different problems. Some were simply annoyances that made it difficult to keep things running smoothly, like the situation with one of my residents,

Kate LaGuardia. She was introduced as the granddaughter of New York City's legendary Fiorello of the same last name, who was mayor during World War II. Kate LaGuardia had arrived at Cornell about the same time I did and was greeted as a celebrity, with a press conference complete with photographers flashing away. And she'd acted like a celebrity ever since, shunting off her duties to younger residents and treating the nurses and the clinic registrar like they were her own private staff. I thought of saying something but decided to let it be. More serious issues required my attention.

One of those was AIDS.

We'd just given the AIDS virus its name in 1982, soon after its emergence. Most medical professionals at first believed that it was a disease that almost exclusively struck drug abusers and gay men. Now, however, we were seeing women in the clinic who were infected. There was no treatment; the virus was essentially a death sentence. When I had such a patient, I'd refer her to one of Cornell–New York Hospital's infectious disease specialists. Those specialists were scratching their heads about how to deal with AIDS, but they were very serious about searching for ways to at least maintain the quality of life for many of these patients.

When things really got strange in the clinic was when a pregnant AIDS patient needed to deliver by cesarean. We had to take precautions, but you could see the incipient hysteria about the disease in the way some medical team members suited up for the OR. They wore OR hoods. They wore boots. They wore triple gloves, triple masks, and triple gowns. Some of them looked like they were landing on the moon to deliver a patient with AIDS. Considering how hot it can get when you're delivering a baby under normal circumstances, it was no surprise that some moon-suited delivery room staff complained of feeling faint. It would be a few years before the fears died down. Nobody knew much yet about the transmissibility of the disease, and no one wanted to find out the hard way.

Not all clinic issues were so intense. One situation had gone on for years, simply because no one had thought to address it: twice a day, patients were herded into the waiting room like cattle. The custom had always been to give all patients the same appointment time, either 8:30 a.m. or 1:00 p.m.

Because of this block scheduling, we could have as many as forty women show up at once, take numbers, and wait for hours until a resident could see them.

I thought of my mother. She'd been a clinic patient when she was pregnant with me, back in 1947. I hated to think of her being treated like that, just another member of the cattle herd; unworthy, in the eyes of those seeing her, of the tiniest concern for her own schedule.

I couldn't change the way Mommy had been treated, but I had the authority to change attitudes at that moment in the New York Lying-In Clinic. As long as this former clinic baby was director, all clinic patients would be treated with respect.

I huddled again with Luradine Timberlake. With three or four residents and four examining rooms, we decided we could schedule four women for 8:30 a.m., three for 8:45, and so on, just like a private practice.

That, as I said, was one of the easy fixes. Some problems proved to be more resistant to change.

Physicians in private practice who had hospital and surgical privileges were on rotation as attending physicians in the clinic, just like those of us who were full-time faculty. While the residents did most of the hands-on patient care, the attending physician—the attending, for short—had the final word and ultimate responsibility for any patient's treatment. That's as it should be. Residents, although they've graduated from medical school, are still in training in their chosen specialty and are not yet qualified to practice solo.

The prior clinical director had taken the job when she was fresh out of the residency program and had not been prone to making waves. So private practitioners with hospital privileges had become accustomed to skipping clinic duty with impunity.

When Grace Sullivan, the clinic nurse director, first told me that many of these physicians were shirking this essential duty, I nearly fell off my chair.

"What do you mean, 'The attendings aren't showing up'?" I asked. "They *have* to show up."

Where I trained, both at Columbia and Roosevelt, attending physicians thrived on teaching. In the military, too, at Bethesda, physicians were eager to pass along their knowledge. The voluntary staff, though, ensconced in their plush Park Avenue offices, were different—as I was discovering.

These were New York City's finest OB-GYNs: powerful doctors who treated the rich, famous, and pampered. I imagine some of them felt that taking care of poor people in the clinic was beneath them. But when they didn't show, who was supervising the residents? Nobody. In the attendings' absence, the residents trained themselves.

something to prove

It seemed that there was nothing I could do to force them. They were called "voluntary" staff for a reason. And they always had excuses when I had my secretary, Mrs. Kiman, call.

But the excuses boiled down to one thing: let the residents fend for themselves.

Not on my watch. I didn't know exactly how I was going to get these private physicians to come in but I knew I had to do it.

I took the problem to the chairman.

"Dr. Ledger, this is a teaching hospital," I said. "How are we going to talk to the residency review committee about our residents being trained properly in outpatient care and ambulatory care when there's no attending supervising them?"

He seemed as surprised as I'd been and agreed that something had to be done.

And then he told me something I hadn't known before: it's a condition of the private physicians' admitting and operating room privileges that they teach in the clinic.

Maybe, I thought, I had some leverage after all.

I spoke to each one of the absentee private practitioners individually, one attending to another:

"Doctor, I've noticed that you have not come to clinic."

Each one recited his excuses. I said I understood, but they still needed to come to clinic. They had an obligation to the residents. It wasn't much of a time commitment, I reminded them, only one morning or one afternoon session a week.

Each of them agreed when we spoke on the phone. But when it came time to precept the clinic, they never showed up. I was beginning to consider the "nuclear option," but before

I took any drastic steps against these very powerful men I needed a paper trail.

So I instituted a new rule: All attending physicians would have to sign in at my office in a book next to the desk of my secretary. That elicited a lot of grumbling but they did it. And knowing that I was keeping tabs convinced more of them to write their clinic time into their schedules in indelible ink. Mrs. Kiman reported back to me that this doctor and that doctor had signed in and the residents were being supervised.

From about ten attendings who never showed, I was down to about four hard cases. They came a few times and then, just stopped again.

It was time to haul out the big guns.

I told Dr. Ledger what I planned, showed him the sign-in sheets with all the blank spaces next to names and asked if he'd back me when the volunteer attendings came to him to complain.

The residents need to have oversight, he said. "Do what you have to do."

I called the OR. "If Dr. Nathanson calls to book a case, you are not to book him," I said. I then rattled off the names of three others who had failed to meet their responsibilities in the clinic and canceled their operating room privileges as well. "And if you have a problem, you can call Dr. Ledger."

Private practitioners make much of their money from operating room and admitting privileges. It wasn't long before the repercussions began. Doctors who had not been challenged about much of anything since they went into practice were howling complaints, squawking "How dare you?" in the general direction of those who told them they weren't getting their way, and were ready to blow through the roof.

Luradine, on the front lines, had to sit politely and smile as a rotund, self-important little man demanded to know who this new clinic director thought she was, that she could tell him what to do. That was one of the tamer responses. I learned secondhand that others on my lost-privileges list called me a "black bitch" and every other derogatory name under the sun. The residents passed along what these angry practitioners had to say about me. So did the nurses. So did the clinic staff.

But I didn't hear a word of complaint from the physicians themselves. When we passed each other in the sub-basement, they were just as polite and nice to me as can be. And we *did* pass each other in the sub-basement because, from then on, they *did* show up for clinic—begrudgingly, for sure.

But they showed up.

Fine with me. As my Daddy would say, I wasn't there to be loved. I had a job to do. And so did they.

One afternoon in that spring of 1983, I was summoned to the chairman's office. On the rare occasions he wanted to see me, I felt as if I was getting called to the principal's office. I wondered, what did I do wrong now?

I took the elevator upstairs from the sub-basement and waited in the reception area until he called me in.

"You've been accepted into the New York Obstetrical Society," he said, smiling pleasantly. "I thought you'd want to know."

He thought I'd want to know? Wow. You bet I did. With news like that, I'd gladly get called to the principal's office every day. I was ecstatic, shocked, thrilled. If he were anyone else, I might have been tempted to give him a big hug. As it was, I thanked him profusely for telling me and then left, my feet barely touching the ground as I walked back to the elevator.

I WAS STILL FLYING high when I got home that night and told Shearwood that I'd been accepted. The news would have been even sweeter if I could have shared it with the two people who were most responsible for everything I had achieved until then, my mother and father, but they were both gone.

I still hadn't quite come to terms with the sudden, unexpected loss of Daddy, and that loss opened up the old wounds of losing Mommy, too.

It again brought to mind something my mother had said to me about six months before she died. In 1976, I was chief resident in OB-GYN at Roosevelt Hospital. I had one of those rare lulls in my work day and took the opportunity to call home, just to see how she was doing. After a bit of small talk, she told me how proud she was of me and of my other sisters. Nobody would have expected much from five little nappy-headed girls who came out of the projects, she said. But there we were, each successful in her own way.

And out of the blue, Mommy said, "Yvonne" (she called me my given name, not my nickname of Cookie, like Daddy did), "it would be nice to have a book in the library, to let everybody know that with faith, persistence, and focus, if you have a dream, you can just follow it, no matter how rich or poor you are."

I agreed that a book would be nice, and prepared to change the subject, but Mommy kept at it. She told me she had made notes about all our lives, starting with how she and Daddy had first met. She seemed to be getting more enthusiastic as she went on about our family's improbable path.

I tried to tamp down her enthusiasm, reminding Mommy that I was often too busy delivering babies to sleep, much less write a book. I just didn't have the time to think of such things.

"Well, it would be nice to have a book in the library," she reiterated.

And that was that. We never spoke of it again. Six months later, she was dead of a stroke, a complication from treatment meant to regulate her heart rate.

It was a total shock. She wasn't supposed to die so young. Although Daddy was the motor, Mommy was the rudder. I thought of how good she'd always been to us, the steady, quiet voice of reason, sacrificing her comfort for the sake of her daughters' future. What could I have done to show my appreciation? She must have had so many dreams that never had been fulfilled.

I knew that her greatest regret in life was that she had had to drop out of Bluefield State Teachers College in her senior year because she didn't have the money for tuition and the school didn't allow seniors to work. Until then, Mommy had paid her school bills by acting as a scrub maid in the school's kitchen. She'd often spoken of being brokenhearted that she'd missed her chance to graduate, after getting straight As in school.

It was too late to fulfill her greatest wish; a college degree was now forever beyond her reach.

But maybe there was something else I could do for her. She'd wanted a book written about our family. A book in the library.

I told my parents' story to a newspaper journalist and a few months later, on Father's Day, 1977, an article ran in the Family/Style section of *The New York Times* about Daddy and his daughters. "A Janitor Who Dreamed That His Daughters Would Be Doctors."

The next thing I knew, a Hollywood producer who had read the article wanted to do a movie about us.

Columbia Pictures swooped in, and suddenly we had stretch limousines parked on our modest suburban street in Long Branch, New Jersey. They recruited a writer from *Good Times,* one of the top television shows of the day, to write the screenplay, and Henry Winkler of Fonzie fame (from television's *Happy Days*) was somehow involved as well.

I told Daddy about Mommy's wish for a book in the library and we went back to the producers and told them a movie was all well and good, but we wouldn't sign anything unless a book was part of the contract.

So they got us a publisher. Frank Conroy, the author who was going to write the book, came out to Long Branch, where he spent days and days interviewing Daddy before he went on to interview me and my other sisters—everyone except Linda, who was in the Army and deployed overseas.

We were on our way to fulfilling my mother's wish when the producer of the movie version, David Begelman, was accused of embezzling from Columbia Pictures.

Everything Begelman had a hand in was immediately scrapped. The limousines were good and gone from our street, never to return. And Mommy's book was never written, let alone published.

I gave birth to Woody in May of 1978. Between becoming a new mom, training for my subspecialty in maternal-fetal medicine, and seeing patients, I had so much to juggle that the whole book idea dropped from my consciousness.

But now, years later, after Daddy died, I thought about Mommy's wish again and wondered if I could make it come true. It would be a way to keep their memory alive and pertinent.

I called Columbia Pictures and asked to be released from the contract we'd signed so I could move on to get a book written. The attorney there said no. Columbia still owned an option that allowed the company to revive the project any time until March 1986, and they weren't going to hand over the rights before that time.

I thanked her and put the expiration date of Columbia's option on my calendar, knowing that they would probably forget about our project as soon as the telephone conversation ended. I'd waited this long. I could wait a little longer.

AT WORK, I WAS still busy with the application to join the FDA trials of the chorionic villus sampling device. In the spring of 1984, Cornell became the eleventh facility the federal agency approved. And I was the hospital's lead investigator.

It was a coup for Cornell and a feather in my cap. Despite all that had happened up to this point, I believed that Drs. Druzin and Ledger would have to acknowledge my value—if not immediately, then eventually. If they were honest with themselves, I thought, they'd see that what I was doing for Cornell negated any preconceptions.

I never let anyone see that the stress was getting to me. I

dealt with it as I had in the past: using food for solace. I got into the habit of stopping for fast food on the way home. At Blimpie's, I'd order a "Blimpie's Best" to eat immediately, and another one to go.

Before long, I was starting to look like a "blimpie" myself. I remember one day wearing a navy blue A-line sailor dress to the office when one of my patients innocently asked, "Dr. Thornton, when are you due?"

After one particularly difficult day at work, I was in bed, watching TV, my trusty bowl of strawberry Häagen-Dazs on the night table, when a commercial for Fred Astaire Dance Studios came on.

I could swear the announcer was talking directly to me:

"Are you bored? Do you feel depressed and unappreciated? Come to Fred Astaire Dance Studios..."

I watched the dancers glide around the dance floor and wanted to join them right then and there. The commercial said that no partner was necessary; they had professional instructors to guide students. I thought, this could be exactly what I needed. And it was exercise, to boot, something to offset the Blimpies and ice cream.

I went the following night, and didn't even tell Shearwood where I was headed because I wasn't sure I'd like it. The moment I opened the door, I knew I was where I needed to be. There was music playing—the Pointer Sisters, "Jump"—mirrors adorned the walls and a big gorgeous ballroom with impeccably dressed dancers in different sections. Some were doing line dances, others did the tango or cha-cha. Someone saw me hesitating at the entrance and shouted, "Come on in!" So I did.

With my musical background, I took to it immediately. My instructor, Tom Roberts, seemed surprised that I picked up the steps so quickly. I left the dance studio that night feeling alive, joyous, and just wonderful. As the song goes, I could have danced all night. It was exactly the therapy I needed.

From then on, Tuesdays and Thursdays were my dance nights. When I told Shearwood before my second lesson though, he wasn't exactly supportive.

"Why do you need to take lessons and spend money?" he asked. "Black people know how to dance."

I said, sure, we know how to dance, but this is different. You need to take lessons to learn proper posture, balance, and dance frame; to learn how to follow your partner, whether in American or International style.

From his expression, you'd think I'd just told him I was planning a vacation on Mars. But that was one of the many benefits of having my own income. Nobody had to understand but me.

After a month, my instructor asked if I wanted to enter a competition. I wasn't ready then, but six months later I agreed. At my first dance competition, in Atlantic City, we won first prize for the cha-cha in the beginners' Bronze category.

I'VE NEVER AGREED WITH those obstetricians who let others take care of their patients during most of the labor and show up just in time for the big event. I believe it's the obstetrician's duty to be at the hospital when the patient arrives. Any patient of mine knew I'd be there to take her step-by-step, through every contraction, along the path to becoming a mother.

But it isn't always that easy when you're a mother yourself.

At home with my two little ones, the same scene played out over and over. The phone would ring. Mrs. Jones, or maybe her husband, would say she's in labor; I'd tell them, "Go to the hospital; I'll meet you there." And then I'd have to tell Woody and Kimmie I was going.

"Mommy has to leave, kids," I'd say. "Be back soon."

"Mommy, where are you going?"

"Mommy has to go to the hospital to deliver a baby."

"Please don't leave us, please don't leave us." And then the tears would start running down their cheeks.

Woody and Kimberly would cry especially hard if I got a call around dinnertime. That was their time to be with me, and to them it must have seemed terribly unfair, knowing that once I walked out the door I wouldn't come home to them for hours and hours.

I'd try to keep it light and happy—"Love you. See you soon."—but seeing their weepy little faces as I left made me feel like something had physically reached into my chest and given my heart a vicious twist.

Pulling out of the garage, I'd see those faces again, now smacked against the family room window, their little noses running and their eyes all red, watching me roll down the driveway.

I'd pretend not to notice that they were upset. I'd wave and smile. And then I would cry my own eyes out as I drove up the hill from the house.

After a while I put my dilemma to the Big One: *God, you've got to do something, this is terrible. I can't keep doing this. There has to be another way.*

something to prove

I'd studied hard all my life. I was a good obstetrician, I was taking care of my patients, but I was also a mom.

What am I going to do? I asked. Just tell me what to do.

I truly believe I got an answer because when the solution came to me, it seemed so obvious, it was like I was being directed to say it. And I knew it would work.

The kids' favorite Saturday morning cartoon characters were He-Man and his sister She-Ra, two super-heroes who would go off to do battle with evil forces whenever someone needed their help. Woody loved He-Man and Kimberly adored She-Ra.

I sat the kids down and asked, "Do you know He-Man? Do you know She-Ra?"

I had their full attention. Yes, they knew He-Man and She-Ra, they answered.

I said, "You know She-Ra goes out and she helps people in trouble because they need her, and she takes care of their needs. Right?"

I explained that when my patients called me on the telephone, it was a call from people who need me, just like the call She-Ra gets when people need her.

"And does She-Ra stay at home?" I waited a beat for them to get what I was saying, then answered my own question. "No, she has to leave to help people, just like He-Man has to help people."

After that talk, it was as if I had waved a magic wand. The next time the telephone rang and I had to leave, Woody and Kimmie were my biggest cheerleaders and said, "Go ahead, Mom! Take care of it, Mom! See you later, Mom!"

I really did feel like a superhero. And, wonder of wonders, they never cried at my leaving again.

WOODY AND KIMBERLY had been going to Helping Hands Nursery School in Hackensack, but in the fall of 1984 it was time for Woody to start first grade in Teaneck, at the public school. I'd kept Woody at Helping Hands through kindergarten because it had a full-day program and public school offered only a half-day of school. Keeping him at Helping Hands an extra year meant that either our baby-sitter or Shearwood or I could pick up the kids from school after work, but it also meant that Woody, who was bashful by nature, felt like an outsider when starting first grade. Everyone else knew each other from kindergarten. On one of his first math tests he did very poorly, and that made him feel even more out of step with the other kids.

So his dad, Shearwood, who is a whiz at this stuff, started helping Woody with his math assignments. Both Woody and Kimberly were coached to memorize the multiplication tables up to 12.

Something clicked, and Woody just sailed through the rest of the year. He finished all the problems in the first-grade math book, then went right through the second-grade math book, and by the end of first grade he had finished the third-grade math book, too. After starting off as one of the worst in his class in math, Woody went on to become the school's first-grade math star.

I think that was the first evidence that we saw of how driven our little boy was to succeed. We knew he had a great memory. He was reading at two years of age, had memorized all the state capitals and could recite "*The Night Before Christmas*" and "*Annabelle Lee*" by age three.

Kimberly, two years younger than Woody, was the gregarious child who easily grabbed the spotlight with her charm and antics. Woody, studious and serious, didn't immediately call attention to himself. His successes would do that for him.

When he started second grade, in September 1985, he was one of the two outstanding students who his teacher, Ms. Bette Kelly, pointed out to the rest of the class. Woody was the brain, the kid who was two years ahead of the rest of the second grade in math; and Kevin Satin, the other student introduced by Ms. Kelly, was the hockey champ, the captain and leading goal scorer of the little league version of the New Jersey Devils. Everyone knew of Kevin Satin who, according to the buzz, was going to grow up to join the pros one day.

These two standouts of the second-grade class became curious about each other and introduced themselves soon after. And thus Woody, slowly and shyly, began to develop his most important boyhood friendship, one that would affect him for the rest of his life.

WE'D GIVEN IN TO Woody's pleas for a Nintendo game. It seemed at first like just another toy so we said, "Sure, why not?"

Shearwood usually got home first and either picked up the kids at school or took over for our nanny, Pam. Between my academic responsibilities and faculty practice, and being on call, my schedule was more jam-packed than my orthopedic surgeon husband's and was also less predictable. Babies come when they come; hip replacements get scheduled weeks or months in advance.

Arriving home tired from the hospital one day, I popped in on Woody and Kimmie, who were downstairs in the family room, playing with their electronic games.

"Hi, kids, what are you doing?"

Nothing. No hello, no nod, no reaction whatsoever. They sat there like little zombies, mesmerized by their Nintendo. All they could see was the monitor and the electronic image of a red race car pinging around an animated blue track.

I wasn't thrilled to be treated by my own children as if I didn't exist. So I stepped in front of the monitor.

"Move, Mom," came the urgent plea, "Get out of the way!"

I did as he asked but as I made a U-turn behind them, and saw how entranced Woody and Kimmie were, I wondered how such a game could possibly be good for them.

I went back upstairs and told Shearwood that I didn't want Nintendo to turn our children's brains to mush.

He smiled and told me to relax, it's just a game. And kids need to play games.

He had a point. It's a game. Kids need to play games. But did they have to play with *that* game?

Just as I'd done in my studies and my career, I'd fallen back on my parents' wisdom when raising my children. They always thought years ahead to how their daughters' childhood activities could help or hinder them as adults. So I tried to think ahead too. One day, they'd be applying for college. No matter how adept they became at it, Nintendo wouldn't impress anyone in admissions.

something to prove

What would help my children develop, do well, and also have fun? They had started piano lessons when they were still toddlers and loved it. What sort of game would make all of us happy?

I finally came up with just the thing: chess. Maybe Kimmie was still too young for it but chess would challenge Woody and stimulate his intellect.

Just one problem: I didn't know how to play chess. Neither did Shearwood. So I put an ad in the paper, "Chess teacher wanted to teach seven-year-old."

The following Sunday, a few days before Christmas, the doorbell rang. I opened it and found a cherubic, shy young man on the doorstep, carrying a composition book. He said his name was Aviv Friedman, he'd just come to this country from Israel, and he lived on the next block, about five houses away.

"I'm an Israeli chess champion," he told me. "My sister saw this ad in the paper."

I told him to come right in, then I took him downstairs to the family room where I had a large black coffee table specially made with an inlaid chessboard. I introduced him to Woody, showed them the wooden chess pieces, and left them alone. As I walked up the stairs, I could hear Mr. Friedman telling Woody that the piece in his hand was a pawn and it was worth one point.

At the end of an hour, I checked on them and I could swear that Woody seemed as engrossed in those little chess pieces as he had been in the dizzy pinging, flashing, and zooming of his Nintendo games.

As I paid Mr. Friedman for the lesson and arranged for

him to come the following week, he said, "You know, your son has a spark."

Even better, Woody said he'd had fun. He was looking forward to his next lesson.

Hearing that was like getting an early Christmas present.

AT WORK, WE'D DECORATED not just the private practice office but the clinic too, with all sorts of holiday glitz and glitter. I was proud of how we'd improved the clinic, and everyone's morale seemed to be way up from what it had been when I'd started.

I had an open-door policy so the staff knew they could come to me with any concerns. The nurses, who were closest to the patients, proved to be bottomless wells of good ideas for improving the clinic. I wasn't always able to get the powers-that-be to agree to our suggestions, but the nurses, clinical assistants, and residents sensed that I was on their side and told me so. And I appreciated their commitment to our patients. We were like a little family down there in the sub-basement.

Toward the end of December, the OB-GYN Department had its own holiday party, upstairs, but I wanted to show my gratitude to everybody who had pitched in to make things run so smoothly. So, at the end of the day, after the last patient had gone, we had a party, just for the clinic staff and the residents. After we exchanged our Secret Santa gifts and toasted the holidays from a large bowl of punch, I handed out printed lyric sheets of some of my favorite carols. I'd brought my guitar with me for the party, took it out of its case, and started to strum. Music was an important part of my life. I'd spent my weekends during much of my childhood and teen years playing gigs with The Thornton Sisters. I wanted to share the gift of music with these people with whom I shared so much during our work day. As I plucked the opening chords of my favorite Christmas song, a few of the staff joined me in singing:

O, holy night, the stars are brightly shining
It is the night of the dear savior's birth...

Pretty soon, everyone was singing along. About the time we began, "What Child Is This?" someone mentioned that, back when she was young, they used to carol throughout the hospital.

"Let's do it," I said, and the whole party moved upstairs, singing all the way.

We started at the top floor, in the labor and delivery area. We skipped the part of the floor where women were actually in labor. When you're in the middle of contractions, about the last thing you want to do is burst out singing.

As we caroled "Silent Night" and "The Twelve Days of Christmas," patients began to join in. You could just see the twinkle in everybody's eyes.

Some of the residents added their voices, and so did some visitors.

We climbed down the stairs to the next floor, caroling all the way, and then the floor after that. By the time we got all the way back to the sub-basement, we'd sung our way through the entire hospital, laughing and sharing the spirit of the season with friends and colleagues, patients and strangers.

It was a lovely moment, the kind that makes you feel that we are all one community and our differences are irrelevant, a moment you can't help feeling wistful about later as you look back and wonder why it can't always be this way among people of good will.

WOODY WAS DOING WELL with his chess lessons. He seemed to have a gift for the game and soon, Mr. Friedman said, if he kept at it, he would be ready to compete in chess tournaments.

Woody also had become closer to the other star of the second grade, his friend Kevin, the Little Jersey Devils' hockey champ. Kevin showed Woody how to score on the ice and Woody taught Kevin how to corner the king on the chessboard and call, "Check."

Of course, the two boys challenged each other to games on Nintendo, too. And Kimmie and Woody still played video games together.

I could deal with that as long as I knew they were engaged in other, more productive activities. I even got Woody an electronic chess game that he could play between his lessons with Mr. Friedman.

The computerized chess game had this annoying mechanical voice that would announce at the end of the game, *"I win. You lose."*

How Woody hated to hear that announcement.

He would play against the machine for hours only to hear, *"I win. You lose."*

It frustrated him to no end.

Then one day, Woody beat the computer. At the end of the

game, the annoying computer-generated voice had a different message: *"I lose. You win."*

Woody was so pleased with himself, he left the game on for hours after that. Anyone going down to the family room would hear the game's mechanized concession of defeat in broken record mode:

"I lose. You win ... I lose. You win ... I lose. You win ..."

chapter four

Mommy's Wish;
Daddy's Voice

*"A lot of people used to say 'What are you doing here,
working on Sunday?' I used to say, 'I eat on Sunday,'
and that would shut them right up."*
                              —DONALD THORNTON

WINTER BLEW THROUGH AND then it was the beginning of spring again.

That spring, I had another reason for feeling a sense of renewal. There, on my calendar, was the notation that Columbia Pictures' option on my family's story was set to expire. That meant I could get the rights back and again work on fulfilling my mother's dream of a book in the library.

I had no idea where to find someone who could help me write the book. I had all the information, but I needed someone who knew how to present it well. I placed an ad in *The New York Times* and contacted a service called Dial-A-Writer. The head of Dial-A-Writer, Dorothy Beach, sent me candidate after candidate and I began interviewing people, looking for the one who could help me tell my story. After a few months of this, I hadn't found the right person. Several of the writers seemed to want to make the story into something it was not. Others seemed remarkably unskilled with the English language for writers, and Mommy, who had studied to be an English teacher before a lack of money forced her to drop out, would never have approved. One whom I thought was talented and bright wanted a small fortune to write the tale.

Dorothy Beach promised to keep trying.

It was fall of 1986 when I met her next recommendation, Jo Coudert. The woman who came to my office at Cornell wore a tan trench coat with a little matching hat, and was very soft-spoken. I guessed her age as about sixty. She didn't bring a tape recorder, she just sat there and listened to my story and every so often she would write in her little steno pad. I think it was about four hours before she offered her opinion on what I'd told her.

"This would be a good human interest story for the *Reader's Digest.*"

Mommy had always liked the *Reader's Digest.* But the *Reader's Digest* wasn't a book.

THAT FALL, KIMMIE BEGAN attending public school too, in first grade. Woody entered the third grade and he and his friend Kevin became even closer. They may have looked an unlikely pair, the jock and the brain, but they connected in a way that only children can, without the judgment that adults layer onto relationships. As close as he was to his sister—and they had always been devoted to each other—in some ways, Woody might have been even closer to Kevin.

Meanwhile, Woody had started complaining about taking music lessons. I told him to keep at it, sure that he'd thank me one day. He insisted that no, he just wasn't that interested any-more, but he took his lessons every Saturday morning, along with his sister, who couldn't get enough of the piano.

Although his enthusiasm for music was ebbing, he had become as obsessed with chess as he'd been with Nintendo. Mr. Friedman agreed that Woody was ready to enter his first tournament.

It was the Pee-Wee Tournament in Washington Township and I made certain that my schedule was clear so I could take him. I sat, did my needlepoint, and watched, understanding almost nothing of the game, as he played against other kids for what seemed like many hours. At last, it was over and Woody had won a trophy. He was so proud of himself, almost as proud as I was of him.

Of course, when Woody came home with his new trea-sure, Kimmie's eyes lit up. Pretty soon, she was taking chess lessons, too.

THE WRITER, JO COUDERT, called to tell me that *Reader's Digest* liked the story. It was going to run in the February 1987 issue. I was getting used to my scaled-down hopes about fulfill-ing Mommy's dream. I'd done my best and maybe this would have to be enough.

One afternoon I was sitting in my office when my secretary,

something to prove

Mrs. Kiman, buzzed me. A box had been delivered from E. P. Dutton, the publisher that had, back in 1978, been recruited by Columbia to publish the book version of the movie they had planned.

The return address showed the editor's name, Tom Congdon. Inside were dozens of audiocassettes. I called him to ask what this was about.

The publisher was going out of business, he said. As he was sorting through some old files, he came across these tapes. They were the ones that Frank Conroy, the author who was supposed to write the book back in 1978, made of the interviews with Daddy and me.

"I met your dad," said Congdon, "He seemed like a great guy. We were just going to throw these tapes away, but I thought you might like to have them."

I thanked him and hung up. I picked up one tape, then another, then set them back in the box. I wasn't ready yet to listen. I certainly couldn't do it there, in the office. I knew that I'd bawl my eyes out, and I had work to do. But I went through the day with my heart pinging around in my chest.

I took the box home with me but still couldn't place the tapes in the cassette player. It had been almost four years since I'd heard Daddy's voice, four years since he died. And although in one way I wanted to hear him again more than anything, in another I knew it would bring back the incredible sense of loss.

I can't tell you how long it was until I got up my courage, but at last I put the first tape in the player, and I heard him again, and I just sobbed and sobbed. He was there in the room with me, his strength, his stubbornness, his wisdom, and his struggles to care for us.

I listened as he talked about moving his family out of the projects in Harlem and back to New Jersey to keep us safe from crime. And how he applied for a job at Fort Monmouth so he wouldn't have to spend what little he earned on commuting.

"...so I went over to dig ditches, but I didn't care what it was. So long as I was close to home."

I listened as he explained how, when he told one of his bosses that he was working a second job so he could save some money to put us girls through college, that boss changed his hours, forcing him to give up the extra work.

And how it took him more than four years to build our house in Long Branch, New Jersey, brick by brick, cinderblock by cinderblock, with building materials he bought every time he had a little extra money.

As I listened, I learned that, in spite of all the prejudice that had been directed toward him throughout his life, the incident that hurt him most involved my youngest sister, Rita. We had been leaving a diner where we'd stopped on the way to a Thornton Sisters gig. It was somewhere in Virginia. Nobody told Daddy what had happened until we were already in the car and on our way.

"It hurt me so bad, I almost cried...Some guy in the diner spit right into Rita's tea...it was four white guys."

I could almost feel the pain he must have felt, hearing that. Daddy was always so protective. We needed him to keep on protecting us as we grew up, but standing up to four racists in a diner on the edge of the South wouldn't have been a wise move in the 1960s for a black man. If Daddy had known what they'd done and confronted the men, who knows what they might have done to him?

I don't know what touched me most, learning things about my parents' lives I'd barely understood growing up, or hearing how much love and thought he put into raising us, his daughters.

"They knew all the things I explained to them in life, no matter how they fall, they can always grab on. If I told them to reach for the moon, and they never got it, they knew in falling they could grab a star. That's the kind of thoughts I would give them."

All the things in life that he could never have, because of his skin color, his lack of education, and the time in which he lived, he wanted to give to us. He sacrificed and worked so the moon and the stars might be within our reach. Both Mommy and Daddy did that. They would always answer their brothers and sisters or co-workers who exhorted, "You work so hard, you are going to kill yourself" with "I'd rather work hard and kill myself than not work hard and have my kids go through what I had to go through."

WHEN THE ARTICLE, "Donald Thornton's Magnificent Dream," appeared in the *Reader's Digest,* so many people told me how much they loved it. Nobody was more excited than I was, though. Jo Coudert had perfectly captured what I'd hoped to convey. Because we all had busy lives, I didn't think much about it when I didn't get any feedback from my sisters. I assumed that they'd all be as thrilled as I was. Well, maybe not all: Jeanette had always been the contrarian of the family and I'd long ago stopped trying to guess her reactions on anything.

My other sisters, though? They'd react as I did, I thought. I wouldn't learn otherwise until much later.

I knew that I needed to do more to tell the story. And now, I knew that Jo Coudert was the writer I wanted to help me do it.

Jo, unfortunately, didn't share my enthusiasm. Before I had the chance to tell her about the tapes, she repeated what she'd said before: I am not writing any book for you.

"If I'm going to write a book, it's going to be my life story, or about whatever I'm interested in, not about somebody else."

I heard her. But I wasn't going to give up. If I'd learned anything from Daddy, it was persistence.

LATER THAT SPRING, Woody came home from school distraught. He and his best friend, Kevin, were now in the fourth grade. They had agreed to work together as a team, competing in a school-wide contest. Whichever team came up with the greatest number of words spelled from the letters that form the word, "constitution," would win a prize.

Woody had been psyched. He was sure they had a good chance of winning. But Kevin confided that he was just too sick to continue. He had to go to Iowa for treatment.

Kevin had leukemia.

I'm not sure how well I hid my shock from my little boy.

I thought of the kid I'd watched sail across the ice, stick in hand, the best little hockey player of the Little New Jersey Devils. Kevin had always been the picture of youthful energy and health.

I didn't want to dismiss the seriousness of his diagnosis, but I didn't want to unduly frighten Woody, either. So we talked about how it was a dangerous disease, but that Kevin was getting the best care possible and that he was a fighter and he'd fight back. For my nine-year-old son, it seemed to be enough.

Shearwood and I, both physicians, understood that Kevin's life might be at risk, but we knew there were good treatments available and kids often pulled through. I wondered, why Iowa? Why not Columbia or Cornell? I figured the treatment might be experimental but Kevin's family was very private and I didn't want to pry.

chapter five

Borrowed Time

*"First, you have to be right with yourself. If you was
to cuss at me, and I was to cuss back to you, there
would be nothing said."*
                                    —DONALD THORNTON

WITH ALL THE CHANGES I'd made at the clinic, we
still could never do the big things. I kept hearing the
same refrain from Dr. Ledger that I'd heard when I first arrived:
no budget.

I'd just about given up begging for most of what we needed
except for the Hoyer lift, a device that helps move very heavy
people from the exam table to a wheelchair or from one table
to another. It was the one thing I kept asking him for. I knew it
was a very expensive piece of equipment, yet I also knew how
badly the nurses needed it.

None of the clinic nurses was a complainer. Even though
it was the mid-1980s, they were accustomed to working in an

area of the hospital that looked like it could have been plucked from the 1930s.

But with our patients getting bigger, the nurses were hurting their backs hefting large women on and off the clinic tables or transferring them to a bed in labor and delivery up on the eighth floor.

So it seemed almost like an answer from heaven when I got a call from someone in Public Relations who informed me that a major corporation was donating $50,000 for the further renovation of the New York Lying-In Clinic.

All I could think was, "Wow! Who could have decided to bestow such a gift?" Nobody even knew we existed, down there in the sub-basement. My best guess was that one of the women from the Ladies Auxiliary, maybe someone who had helped us spruce up the clinic walls and waiting rooms with paintings, was responsible. Maybe our unknown benefactor saw that we needed so much more than the Ladies Auxiliary could provide and suggested to her important executive husband that his company make such a donation.

While I didn't know who to thank, I certainly knew how to use the funds—and not just on the Hoyer lift. We needed new exam tables. We needed better lighting. We needed updated equipment.

The woman from Public Relations told me that the check would be presented in a little ceremony at the Griffis Faculty Club, which was located within Cornell Medical College adjacent to the hospital's main entrance; the Griffis was a sedate, sophisticated, elegant, wood-paneled meeting place, reminiscent of the Harvard Club.

Borrowed Time

Public Relations had alerted the media and I prepared a little speech to give when I accepted the gift on behalf of the hospital.

The day of the event, I took the elevator upstairs to the Griffis Faculty Club, walking past corridor walls lined with the portraits of Cornell's most eminent professors and distinguished faculty from years past.

I got up in front of an audience of about twenty or thirty people, made up mostly of the current elite of Cornell and administrative heads of New York Hospital, along with representatives of our corporate benefactor, and thanked the donor for recognizing the needs of people of lower socioeconomic means.

"With this donation, we can continue to improve the clinic."

My speech was short and sweet. After a few more words of appreciation, I stepped to the right and let the corporate representative presenting the check take over at the lectern.

He whipped out an oversized check made out to the clinic that was more like a banner. It must have been six feet long by two feet high.

Flashbulbs popped from around the room as the media and others took photographs. For just a second, I felt almost giddy thinking about what we could now finally get done.

As the giant award became more unwieldy, the donor motioned to me for help in balancing the oversized check. The room got very still.

It was the crowning moment, when you'd ordinarily expect smiles, laughter, and applause all around. Instead, there was stunned silence from those assembled. They looked taken aback, as if a bad smell had wafted through the air.

something to prove

I looked toward the corporation's representative, just for an instant, unsure of what was causing this reaction in Cornell's old guard. I turned my head back to the crowd. It was then that I saw that scene through their eyes—my black hand on the upper right-hand corner of their oversized photo-op check.

Suddenly, it dawned on me. My face wasn't the image that these very important men wanted representing Cornell.

I kept smiling though, pretending I didn't see the disapproving looks on the faces in the audience and couldn't guess the content of the whispers from one to the other. I let my gaze drift to Luradine Timberlake and one of the other nurses who'd come up from the clinic and whose faces held the only other smiles in the room.

As soon as it was over, I hurried back to my office and called Shearwood.

I gave him the blow-by-blow description of the presentation and said, "Honey, I don't think I'll be director of the clinic for long."

It wasn't that I believed they'd fire me from Cornell, "But they are not going to let me be the public face of anything," I said. "Not after today."

"Come on, there's no reason to think that," Shearwood said. He tried his best to reassure me, but I knew what I'd seen.

A FEW WEEKS WENT by, a month, two months, and things were back to normal at the clinic, only better. We were getting the upgrades I'd tried unsuccessfully to get for years. I'd heard no negative feedback since the check presentation ceremony and despite my initial concerns after the audience reaction during the photo op, there had been no apparent consequences.

I began to relax, figuring that Shearwood had been right. There was no reason to believe the hospital would replace me. Who else, with any credentials, would want to come down to the sub-basement and be director of a clinic? My qualifications were vastly superior to those of any of Dr. Ledger's previous clinic directors. The nurses and the rest of the clinic staff were happier with me at the helm than they'd been in the past. The patients were happier. The clinic was running more smoothly than before I came, and the residents were well supervised.

Even if none of that were enough to persuade him of my value, Dr. Ledger had to know that my efforts were probably what had attracted that big check. It had been slated for "*further* improvements." That meant that whoever decided to give us the money knew that some improvements had already been made, and I was the one who had made them. I knew from Luradine and the other clinic nurses that most or all of my predecessors had never considered trying.

Whether the Cornell elite liked seeing my hand on that check or not, they had to understand that without my efforts, there probably would be no check.

So maybe I had overreacted.

I wasn't going to beat myself up over it. Considering how the chairman and some others had behaved toward me since I first got to Cornell, I figured I was entitled to a bit of paranoia.

I put it behind me and concentrated on my work.

OUR PARENTS HAD WANTED us Thornton sisters to stay close to each other, no matter what. Maybe they had been too successful at their goal of making sure each of us was well educated and could stand on her own because, as we grew in our professions and married, we found ourselves going separate ways. Jeanette and her husband, Emile, had their psychiatric and gastroenterologist medical practices in Albany, New York. Donna, her meteorologist husband, Willis, and their daughter, Heather, lived in Virginia. Linda, in the Army, and married to Roger, a lawyer, traveled the world.

While Rita, our foster sister, Betty, and I all lived relatively close to each other in New Jersey, our busy lives left little time for each other. Once a year though, we tried to continue a tradition of a family picnic in Lakewood, New Jersey's Ocean County Park, where we'd held our family get-togethers since at least 1950.

The rambling, wooded park, that was once the private vacation playground of one of the Rockefellers, covered hundreds of acres. It had a large, lovely lake and plenty of hiking and biking trails. We had so many wonderful memories of picnicking on the sandy beach at the lakefront with Mommy and Daddy that it just seemed right to return to it after they were both gone.

Daddy had always made sure we girls were well stuffed when we were children. I suspect he had dual reasons for this. His family had been very poor while he was growing up during the Great Depression, and as one of the younger children in a big family, he ate oatmeal three times a day. If there were any meat or potatoes to be had, those treats went to his older brothers. Remembering the deprivation of his own childhood, Daddy made sure that all his girls had plenty to eat.

And he had an ulterior motive that he was more than happy to broadcast to anyone who would listen. If his girls were chubby, boys would find us less attractive. So we'd be forced to focus on our studies instead of being dazzled by boys who Daddy worried would get us pregnant and then leave us with no prospects and another little mouth to feed.

Our childhood habits carried over into adulthood, and nowhere was that more evident than at the family picnic. We may have been only fifteen or sixteen people, but we came prepared to cook for an army. We didn't just bring pots of food; we brought vats. The brothers-in-law manned the grill, tossing on the burgers, sausages, and spareribs, while we sisters laid out the picnic table with assorted other goodies: potato salad, fried chicken, chips, and pretzels.

Just once did the topic of the *Reader's Digest* article about Daddy come up, and for the briefest instant I thought I saw a look of annoyance pass between Jeanette and Rita.

Uh-oh. I had no clue what was going on between them but decided not to ask. This was a happy occasion and I intended to keep it that way.

Someone had brought a portable stereo and we danced to "Shotgun" by Junior Walker and the All Stars. The children, with their badminton rackets, ran back and forth on the grass, batting at a shuttlecock.

As diverse as our lives were, at these reunions, it always felt like no time had passed at all.

And then we went our separate ways and the distance intruded again. But this year, something urgent came up that prompted a call from my oldest sister, Donna, after our annual reunion.

Donna's daughter, Heather, was just about ready to start

college. Unlike the rest of the Thornton sisters, Donna wasn't interested in earning a bachelor's degree and hadn't enjoyed much of a professional life. Her husband, Willis, had old-fashioned attitudes about women and work. Donna acquiesced to his wishes to be a stay-at-home mom to Heather. Although she'd worked for a while as a court stenographer, Donna knew that our parents had had bigger dreams for her—and she had bigger dreams for herself. Now that Heather would soon be away at school, Donna imagined herself pursuing some of those deferred dreams. I vaguely knew her situation and was surprised when she called me, in tears.

"Yvonne, my doctor says I have this lupus thing, this terrible thing that's making it difficult for me to breathe," she said. "I need for you to call him."

Donna had always had health problems. She'd suffered with intractable epilepsy and some years later had developed debilitating, Stage IV endometriosis. Now, she was diagnosed with lupus—formally, systemic lupus erythematosus. Lupus, I knew, could be a nasty disease. It's an autoimmune disorder, meaning that the body's immune system becomes confused, sees its own tissues and organs as invading organisms, and launches the kind of defense against them that is supposed to be reserved for foreign substances. Now the lupus was causing Donna's immune system to attack her lungs.

I tried to calm her, telling her that lupus was usually a very manageable illness. Even with this new complication, I said, she shouldn't panic. That didn't do much to assuage her, but I took her doctor's number and promised I'd call him to get a sense of the prognosis.

When I called, I expected to get a nuanced view from her rheumatologist of her symptoms and treatment options that I could communicate to Donna in a reassuring way.

Instead, this physician, very matter-of-factly, with no more sensitivity than I've heard from my car mechanic when telling me I need new brakes, said, "She's going to be dead in five years."

I nearly dropped to the floor. Mommy was gone, Daddy was gone, but my sister couldn't be on that path. Not yet. She was only 43 years old.

I was almost as shocked by his demeanor over the telephone. Couldn't he have found a gentler, more compassionate way to break the news?

Never mind that I was a physician. I was a sister first.

"Excuse me," I said, barely containing my emotions, "would you expound upon that, please?"

"Your sister has interstitial pulmonary fibrosis," he said. "This is a fatal complication of lupus."

I understood what interstitial pulmonary fibrosis was. Scar tissue, formed as a result of Donna's immune system's attack on her lungs, had reduced the lungs' ability to function.

Was this really a death sentence, though?

I wanted to scream at him for his lack of empathy, but I didn't.

Instead, I asked, "How can you be so certain?"

He'd seen similar cases before, he said, and summed up his opinion by reiterating that although he would put her on steroids, with her condition, five years was about all the time she had.

I thanked him and hung up the phone. How was I supposed to relay this to Donna? Could I even be sure this doctor was right?

I wasn't sure, of course. I also knew her physician hadn't told her any of this, so I didn't either. Instead, I said, "Donna, you do have this complication of lupus involving your lungs. But hopefully, with steroids and newer treatments, you will be able to lick this thing." In my heart, I suspected that the rheumatologist was right. But I prayed for the best.

WE DID GET SOME hopeful news on a different front. Woody's friend, Kevin, had returned from getting treatment in Iowa and was in remission from the leukemia.

When he came over to play with Woody, to hide his now-hairless scalp, Kevin wore a brown baseball cap with a Hershey's logo. Other than that, he looked like his old self.

I explained to Woody that chemotherapy could cause hair loss but stressed that it would grow back, good as new. Kevin was on the mend.

Woody was overjoyed to see his friend again and seemed buoyed by Kevin's positive attitude. Kevin was better, that was all Woody knew or needed to know. As the boys went downstairs to the family room to play chess, I felt grateful, for both Kevin's and Woody's sake, that the treatment had worked.

Together again, they were oblivious, as only children can be, to everything but their games. Kevin was about as adept at chess as Woody was at hockey—in other words, not at all—but the boys took pleasure in teaching and learning from each other.

Woody had been steadily improving at his chess game, and

his teacher, Mr. Friedman, said he'd be ready by the end of the year to enter his first rated tournament. Unlike the Pee-Wee tournament he'd entered last year, rated ones attracted highly skilled players of all ages.

ABOUT SIX MONTHS AFTER the check photo-op fiasco, I was in my office, catching up on paperwork, when Luradine Timberlake dropped by and asked if she could have a word with me. She seemed distraught so I told her to come in, have a seat, and tell me what the matter was.

"I don't want you to leave the clinic," she said. "You're the best thing that ever happened to us."

She looked like she was about to burst into tears. I came around the side of the desk to comfort her.

"Luradine, calm down, it's all right," I said. "What gave you the idea that I was leaving?"

She refused to be consoled. The rumors were going around among the residents, she said. They all said that a new director was coming in.

"How can that be? I haven't heard any such thing." I explained that if there were going to be a new director, there would have been memos about the change and Dr. Ledger would have told me before telling anyone else.

Nothing I could say seemed to assuage her. She'd been tearful as she told me all this. Now, she started sobbing.

"Look, I see you're all upset. Let me call Dr. Ledger and we'll get to the bottom of this right now."

I walked around to my side of the desk, picked up the phone and called the chairman.

"Dr. Ledger, this is Yvonne," I said. I told him I was sitting there in my sub-basement office with a very distraught Luradine who kept insisting that I'd no longer be the director of the clinic and no matter how many times I told her she was wrong, she wouldn't believe me because of some silly rumors that were going around.

I expected him to say it was all just a misunderstanding.

His answer was just two words long. Two words that I didn't see coming:

"She's right."

I kept my composure as much as I could and asked if I could come up to his office and discuss this.

"WE'RE HAVING KATE LAGUARDIA take over as Clinic Director," said Dr. Ledger when I met with him.

Kate LaGuardia? She had been my resident. All the clinic staff had complained about her back then because she'd always demanded that they drop whatever they were doing to serve her needs instead.

How could he give her my job? She had just finished her residency and she wasn't even Board-certified. But I guess her notable last name trumped anything that I had to offer.

He sugar-coated it, telling me I was a valuable member of the department but that he wanted me to concentrate on the chorionic villus sampling program and my private faculty practice instead. Never mind that I'd already been doing both along with running the clinic. Dr. Ledger's word was law.

Someone once said that you find your opportunities in the castaway areas of life. The clinic was my opportunity. Now it was being snatched away from me, without consent or discussion. My instincts had been correct, but it still hurt.

I later learned that the entire clinic staff, four nurses, eight clinical assistants, and four registrars, all signed a letter to Dr. Ledger telling him that I'd been the best director the clinic had ever had, and begging him to reconsider his decision to replace me with Kate LaGuardia.

Their letter might as well have never been written.

chapter six

Keep an Eye on the Team for Me

"My life has been my children."
—DONALD THORNTON

D R. KATE LAGUARDIA STILL had a residency to complete in preventive medicine, so she didn't immediately take over as director of the clinic. For me, some of the joy went out of the job, knowing that all I'd accomplished there wasn't worth a damn to Dr. Ledger.

You could sense the drop in enthusiasm among the clinic staff, too. Luradine and the other nurses realized that the new clinic director, who had behaved so imperiously toward them when she was a resident, wasn't likely to listen to their concerns.

Despite my imminent replacement as director of the clinic, I didn't get an office in the OB-GYN Department on the first floor. My office would still be in the sub-basement. And

95

new clinic director Kate LaGuardia's office would be some-where upstairs.

I knew it did no good to brood, though. I tried to imagine Daddy's voice in my head. What would he say if he could see me sitting there, feeling sorry for myself? He'd been through so much worse, and had managed to find ways to survive and even thrive. He'd taken control of what he could control, and I had to do the same.

I'd been steadily gaining weight. That was something I could control and I became determined to reverse course. Instead of seeking solace in food, I found it in my ballroom dancing classes. Dancing made me feel carefree and joyous, and it was also fabulous exercise. I joined Weight Watchers. The pounds began to drop off.

THE NURSES SAW ALL the attendings at our best and our worst. Their own medical knowledge gave them insights into every physician's professional strengths and weaknesses. All the doctors who practiced or had privileges at Cornell were among the best in their fields, of course. But even among this elite assembly, there were differences. And if anyone could rec-ognize those differences, it was the nursing staff, who watched us all in action. So, I felt honored when one of the labor and delivery nurses, Helen Morris, selected me as her OB-GYN, rather than one of the more renowned physicians. It was the kind of affirmation I needed when I was feeling so low.

Helen, a statuesque woman who looked younger than her thirty-two years, arrived at my private practice wearing a tailored taupe pants suit that flattered her trim figure, and tasteful small gold hoop earrings. She had a flawless coffee-colored complexion and a no-nonsense demeanor. She wasn't married but she was in a long-term relationship, and she and her partner had agreed they were ready to have children. Easier said than done.

She had been pregnant three times, she told me. And each time, she had miscarried.

Miscarriages in the first trimester aren't all that unusual. As many as twenty-five percent of pregnancies spontaneously miscarry within the first twelve weeks.

Helen's miscarriages were occurring much later though, toward the end of her second trimester, when she was between twenty-two and twenty-four weeks pregnant. It's heartbreaking to lose a baby at that late stage, when you're past the halfway mark and you've probably already felt the little one kick.

In my assessment of her, I discovered that Helen's problem was a relatively rare condition called cervical incompetence or insufficiency. When the cervix is too weak to hold the growing fetus, it opens before the baby comes to full term. The fetus is expelled too early in development to survive.

Helen wanted very much to be a mother and planned to try again to conceive. She asked if I could help her bring her next pregnancy to term.

I told her I'd be delighted to help but, "It's going to be difficult unless we put a stitch in the cervix."

That stitch would mean minor surgery, and the best time to do it would be after twelve weeks into the next pregnancy.

She had an infection so I prescribed antibiotics and told her to use birth control for the next several weeks. She could think about motherhood again once the infection had cleared.

WOODY BROUGHT KEVIN over to play one day in the spring and I could see that the little hockey star looked wan compared to the last time I'd seen him, some months earlier.

A few minutes of conversation confirmed what I suspected from his appearance. Kevin's leukemia was back with a vengeance.

He was due to go back to Iowa, this time for a bone marrow transplant. With luck, the stem cells in the new marrow would replace the unhealthy ones and Kevin would be good as new. He'd already jumped the biggest hurdle, that of finding a donor who was a perfect match: his little sister, Jennifer. Most people in need of such a match never locate one. The prospects were good, especially for a young boy who had always been physically active and in otherwise good health before being stricken.

Every doctor will tell you that no procedure is foolproof. Before the transplant, Kevin's own bone marrow would have to be completely destroyed by radiation and/or chemotherapy in preparation for the introduction of the new bone marrow stem cells. That made it a hazardous treatment with plenty of possibilities for complications. While I knew he was in for a grueling regimen, I also knew that bone marrow transplants were among the treatments of choice for leukemia. This just might be what would restore him to health.

I was thinking all this when the little hockey star turned to Woody and said something so touching, it stays with me to this day.

Keep an Eye on the Team for Me

"If I don't get back, Woody, just please keep an eye on the New Jersey Devils for me," said Kevin.

I tried to lift his spirits. There was no way that this little kid wasn't coming back to us, and I said so.

Woody chimed in with equal certainty. "What are you talking about? Of course, you're coming back."

"No, well, just in case," he said, "I want you to promise you'll keep an eye on the team for me."

Woody said okay and the boys went downstairs to play.

THE LOSS OF THE directorship of the clinic should have freed up some of my time, but between the chorionic villus sampling program, supervising residents, and seeing patients in my private practice, my workdays were as jam-packed as before.

Shearwood usually picked up Woody and Kimmie at school but when he couldn't make it, our new nanny, Mrs. Hills, would drive to Hawthorne Elementary School and take them home. Because emergencies happen, if neither Shearwood nor Mrs. Hills were available, we taught the children a secret password in case we had to have someone else come for them after school. Shearwood and I were always concerned about our children's safety, knowing that evil forces lurked around each corner, so we picked a password that we figured would be un-guessable: "Ultra-high molecular weight polyethylene."

But I refused to let my schedule interfere when my kids needed me. My mom always said, "No amount of success in your profession can ever make up for being a failure at home," and I took that to heart. Never mind hell or high water—come quintuplets or emergency cesarean, if my own babies needed their mom to show up, I'd find a way to be there.

I remember one time I almost didn't make it. Kimmie had a piano recital at school, and I had been called into the hospital for a first-time mom the previous night after dinner. Unlike the dramas seen on television when a mother-to-be goes into labor, the average time from the beginning of labor until delivery is more than twenty hours for first-time moms. Figuring I was in for an all-nighter and then some, I told Shearwood to go on ahead to Kimmie's recital and I'd meet him there. The recital was set for 2:00. I hoped that my patient would have delivered long before then. Lucky for me, Kimberly told me that she wasn't the first child playing that afternoon, so I had a little wiggle room.

I told my patient, Cindy, that I would be with her all night if that is what it took, but if she hadn't delivered by 1:30 the next afternoon, I would have one of my colleagues, Dr. Lars Cederqvist, take over because, no matter what, I had to be at my daughter's recital. I'd promised.

Cindy didn't like the idea of my leaving before she delivered, but I explained that she'd understand once she became a mom.

By noon the next day, she still hadn't fully dilated and I reminded her I'd have to leave. Whether it was just nature taking its course or a new mother's determination to have her own doctor attend her delivery, things speeded up considerably from there. She soon was fully dilated and she pushed her daughter out in almost record time—a beautiful little girl with a head full of hair. Mother and child began to bond and I got caught up in the joy of the delivery, until Cindy said, "Dr. Thornton, don't you have someplace to go?"

I looked at the clock and panicked. The recital would start in less than half an hour.

With no time to change, I threw my white coat over my scrub dress and hurried out of the hospital.

I raced up the FDR Drive, over the George Washington Bridge, and through the streets of Teaneck, risking speeding tickets all the way. At last, ahead of me, I saw the big old red-brick school building, pulled into the first spot I found in the school parking lot, and began jogging toward the auditorium. I'm not even sure if I remembered to lock the car. Throwing open the schoolhouse doors, I sprinted down the hall, only to find that the auditorium was packed. No way was I going to find a seat in time. Quickly changing direction, I ran around to the back entrance of the auditorium, up the stairs to the back-stage area, out of view of the audience. I waited in the wings, leaning against one of the supports, just as Kimmie, in her pink lace dress and patent leather Mary Jane shoes sat down at the piano bench and flipped through the pages of her music, preparing to play. There must have been two hundred other parents and friends in the audience and she had to have been scouring all those faces, looking for mine, for the last fifteen minutes. I was almost hidden in the corner of the backstage and wasn't able to catch her eye right away. I could see the dis-appointment in her little face as she searched for the page she wanted. Did she believe I had missed her recital? For a second, she looked close to tears.

I don't know whether it was the glare of my white lab coat against all the duller colored props backstage or the sound of my panting after running all that way. But she seemed to sense something, turned her head toward me, and found me smiling back at her. Her face lit up like the footlights of a Broadway theater.

She started playing then, a lively rendition of Bach's "Solfeggietto in C Minor" that she'd been practicing for at least three months with her piano teacher, Mrs. Chou. I was so proud of her. Mostly though, I was relieved I'd arrived in time. Even though I probably left a few skid marks on the school's driveway, it was worth it. I was there when she needed me there. That's all that mattered.

DEVOTED AS THEY ALWAYS were to each other, my children were as different as two siblings could be. Woody took after his father: sturdy, laconic, and stoic. My talkative little Kimmie loved the spotlight, could charm the spots off a ladybug, and had a mischievous, defiant streak that was both adorable and exasperating.

Her propensity for trouble showed up early, when she was still a baby, crawling around the floor at home. She found a hairpin, looked around for something she could do with it, and seemed determined to poke it into an electrical outlet. When I saw what she was about to do, I jumped up, said, "No, no, no, Kimmie!" and tried to divert her attention to something else.

She looked at me, looked at the outlet, and the message in her expression seemed to be, *I'll do exactly as I please.*

I kept coaxing and distracting and she kept crawling back, becoming more obsessed with the outlet the more I tried to thwart her. When it became clear that words couldn't deter her, I resorted to a good swat on the bottom. It was that or risk having my little girl light up like a Christmas tree the next time I turned my back. After that, she realized that sticking hairpins into electrical outlets involved more downside than she was willing to risk. Soon, however, she found other ways to drive her parents crazy.

Sitting in our living room one night, after Kimberly was old enough to walk, Shearwood and I heard a huge thud. It seemed to be coming from Kimmie's room.

We got up to explore. I peeked through the keyhole so we wouldn't get her all excited by opening the door.

As I watched, I saw her climb from the crib up onto the top of the dresser, which was attached to her crib. Then she stood up and dive-bombed back into her bed.

Our first reaction was a simultaneous, *"Oh, my God!"* but we didn't want to make a big deal out of it. So we scolded her, gave her a time-out, and told her it was dangerous and not to do it anymore. We figured that would be the end of it.

A few weeks later, Shearwood was attending a conference out of town. I heard the same thud, followed a moment later by a blood-curdling scream. I raced into Kimmie's room and found her crumpled up in her crib. She had dive-bombed, missed the mattress, and had hit her head on the crib rails. Blood dripped down her forehead, into her eyes, and all over her mint green Winnie the Pooh pajamas.

She was wailing and I was about ready to faint from fright. Yes, as a physician, I see blood all the time—but it's one thing to perform surgery on a patient and quite another to see your own tiny child hurt and bloody. I pulled myself together, cleaned her up with hydrogen peroxide, put some butterfly bandages on the laceration, and called a plastic surgeon friend who calmed me down, told me I did the right thing, and asked me to come to his office with Kimmie the next day.

I figured she'd learned her lesson and wouldn't be doing that anymore.

As she grew, Kimmie didn't become any more subdued. But she was always entertaining. Her teachers called her "The Divine Miss Kim" and she managed to say some unintentionally hilarious things—like the time we were standing in line at a football game to buy hot dogs and she blurted out, "Mommy, what's the difference between a condom and a condominium?"

I quickly explained that one protected you and the other was a place to live, then distracted her with a hot dog. That, fortunately, took her mind off asking any follow-up questions.

She was also about as bright a child as I'd ever come across, and I don't think I'm biased just because she's my daughter. Even Woody, her brother, who already had a reputation as the "brain" in his class, insisted that Kimberly was smarter than he was.

So when I got a call from her school one day, I assumed that my brilliant little daughter, now in the second grade, had won some sort of award, or maybe aced the spelling bee or had otherwise done something to make a parent proud.

Well, no.

I found Kimmie in the principal's office.

"We have a situation, Mrs. McClelland," said the principal. In my professional life, I was Dr. Yvonne S. Thornton, but to the principal and faculty of Hawthorne Elementary School, I was Mrs. Shearwood J. McClelland.

"Kimberly showed her panties to a boy," said the principal. "And we believe that it is not appropriate."

Kimmie looked up at me as if to say, *why all the fuss?*

I promised the principal I'd talk to Kimmie at home and explain to her why she shouldn't do such things.

But Kimmie chimed in, seemingly offended that anyone else was taking offense.

"Well, Brian dared me to do it, Mommy. He dared me."

I told her to let the principal finish speaking and we'd discuss the situation at home, "because you know that Mommy would not approve of you pulling up your dress showing your panties to anyone. No matter what."

"He dared me to do it," she repeated, as if that excused everything. "I'm not going to turn down a dare."

We had a long talk about boys and girls and inappropriate behavior when we got home, and then she was punished. I wondered what type of punishment would be most effective with Kimmie. I thought of what my mother would do in a similar situation. It hurt me more than it did Kimberly, but she received her last spanking that afternoon. To this day, I'm sure she thinks that it was the punishment itself that was inappropriate and that she'd been treated unfairly. But that's my Kimmie.

LATE THAT SUMMER, my patient, Helen Morris, came in to confirm that she was indeed pregnant again. I checked to make sure that the infection she'd had when she first came to see me had cleared. It had; the antibiotics had done their job, and the cultures were all negative. I congratulated Helen and explained the surgery I planned to perform to improve her chances of carrying a healthy baby for nine months, until it was time for delivery. There are two ways of reinforcing or encircling a malfunctioning cervix, I said. The easier, purse-string procedure would leave a little bit of the suture visible outside the cervix. That could possibly invite infection to travel up along the exposed "wick" to the uterus. To be on the safe side, I told her, I planned to do a somewhat more complicated but an ultimately more conservative version of the purse-string procedure known as a Shirodkar cerclage. The suture would be buried, and thus it would not be as prone to infection. Doing the more complex procedure meant that Helen would have to deliver by cesarean, but I felt the approach was best, given her history.

Since Helen was a labor and delivery nurse, she understood my explanation and agreed with my assessment.

Our next step would be to schedule her surgery. Because most miscarriages occur in the first trimester of pregnancy, we'd have to wait until after the first twelve weeks. The timing had to be just right. If we waited too long, she would again risk loss of the pregnancy due to an incompetent cervix. That put us into October.

Helen left the office looking happy and hopeful. And I went on to see my next patient.

THE SCHOOL YEAR was about to begin and Kevin hadn't yet returned. That wasn't surprising, considering the treatment he had undergone. The bone marrow transplant from his little sister, Jenny, seemed to be working. Woody had heard from Kevin over the summer and had learned that much. He couldn't wait to see his best friend but I knew it would take some time, probably several months, before Kevin's bone marrow would function properly again. For those months, it would be important for Kevin to be in an environment where he was closely monitored. The fifth grade of Hawthorne Elementary School definitely was not such an environment.

A few days into the new school year, Miss Nelson, the school nurse, told the fifth-grade teacher that she had an important announcement to share with Woody's class. The teacher herded the thirty or so boys and girls into a quiet area of the school library. Miss Nelson waited for the children to settle down and then, as gently as she could, she told them why she wanted to speak to them.

The treatment that had seemed to hold so much promise for their classmate, Kevin Satin, had failed. The amazing little goal-scorer and MVP of the Little New Jersey Devils, the boy who was supposed to grow up and join the hockey pros, was dead of leukemia. He'd been just ten years old.

Woody came home in shock. He couldn't stop crying and I admit that I cried right along with him.

Even as a doctor, I was unprepared. I specialized in happy events, the joy of bringing new babies into the world and seeing the thrill of the little ones' arrivals in the expressions of the new parents. I rarely dealt with life-threatening illness or death. And now, my own little Woody was experiencing profound grief and loss.

He wanted to know why. I had no answers. All I could do was hold him and kiss him and tell him it was all right, but

I knew my attempts to comfort him could never be enough. Woody had this big hole in his heart and there was no way that I could fill it or make it better or stop it from hurting.

THE FUNERAL WAS AT Vander Plaat Memorial Home in Paramus, about five miles from Teaneck. The simple brick building conveyed a comforting solidity. We walked up its wide steps under a portico flanked by two white columns, and entered a paneled foyer. None of us spoke above a whisper, not even my usually boisterous little Kimmie.

Soft music was playing and we followed it to a room where thirty or forty people stood in small groups or sat here and there on the cushioned wooden chairs lining the center of the room in neat rows. At the door, we found a tray of yarmulkes. In deference to Kevin's faith, Shearwood placed one on Woody's head and positioned a second on his own.

On a green floral camelback sofa along one wall, an older woman sat weeping quietly while a man rubbed her shoulder, his own gaze turned inward and filled with sadness. In front of us, set against a draped wall, was Kevin's casket. Even closed, the sight of it was like a punch in the gut. This, more than any-thing, made Kevin's death real. Woody whimpered. I hugged him and tried to soothe him.

Kevin's mother and father stood near the casket, leaning on one another, two tall, slender people who appeared frag-ile enough to shatter. I'm sure we expressed our condolences before taking our seats but what I said, what Shearwood said, got lost in the fog of sorrow. How does anyone find words that can come within miles of being adequate at a time like this?

In their faces I could see the echo of the child they had lost. He'd had his mother's eyes...his father's smile.

I tried to fathom what they must be going through. It was beyond my understanding.

A few of Kevin's relatives and one of his teachers took turns telling stories about the little boy's spirit, his talent on the ice, his courage through the ordeal of treatment, and his love for his family. His mother spoke briefly and then, his younger sister, Jenny, who had bravely donated her bone marrow, said a few words. One by one, those who loved the young boy said their good-byes. The rabbi said a prayer. Then we all drove to the cemetery and walked behind Kevin's coffin in a slow procession to the grave site. As we passed other graves, I saw that pebbles and small stones had been placed on some headstones, but I didn't know what this meant.

In a final ritual, after the coffin was lowered into the ground, mourners tossed small shovelsful of dirt into the grave. Dozens of people filed by us but all I could see, even when I closed my eyes, was that small white casket.

Woody sobbed through most of the service at the funeral home and now at the burial site. He gripped my hand and we tried to be strong for him. We told him that Kevin was in a better place. He wasn't suffering any longer. And we meant it but, oh, that little casket. Imagining Kevin in there nearly ripped my heart out.

I looked up at my big, strong husband, Shearwood. Tears flowed silently in small rivulets down his cheeks. It was the only time I'd ever seen him cry.

something to prove

WOODY REMAINED TRAUMATIZED AND inconsolable. Mourning the loss of his friend seemed to change him physically, so that his whole body, in his every movement, resounded with sadness. He didn't say much, but what he did say showed that he wasn't letting go. He prayed often that Kevin was in heaven. He asked Shearwood and me for reassurance that his friend would be all right up there, all alone.

He'd come down to breakfast and say, "Mom, this is the fourteenth day since Kevin died." Weeks went by, and he was still marking off the time on the calendar.

"It's the thirtieth day since Kevin died."

After he said his prayers at night, Woody quietly reminded me, "It's the forty-first day, Mom."

I knew that being overwhelmed with grief wasn't healthy for him but I didn't know what to do for him at first.

Months passed. Each day was another that Woody marked off according to that sad before-and-after divide. Finally, I sat him down and said, "I don't believe Kevin would want you to think that way, Woody. I really don't."

As he listened, I could see that he was taking my words to heart, so I went on, as tenderly as I could.

"You're here to continue where Kevin left off," I said. "Didn't Kevin ask you to watch out for the Devils for him if he should not make it back from Iowa?"

Woody agreed that yes, Kevin had asked him to do just that.

"So he wants you to live," I told him. "He wants you to be happy. And I don't think counting the days since he's been gone is going to help make you feel any better."

He thought about that for a while. And, at last, he stopped

marking each new day as a commemoration of Kevin's death. Instead, he threw himself into learning about professional ice hockey. Soon, he was a walking encyclopedia on the sport ... especially The New Jersey Devils.

chapter seven

Can I Still Have a Baby?

*"If there's a heaven and hell on earth, then
I've been to heaven, see, because I'm happy.
I've never hurt nobody."*
                    —DONALD THORNTON

HELEN MORRIS GOT THROUGH her first trimester without a hitch, and in her thirteenth week we were ready to do her procedure. I suited up, entered the OR, and scrubbed. The head circulating nurse, a woman who had been at Cornell forever, had been responsible for prepping Helen for surgery. The anesthesiologist asked Helen to count backward from one hundred. I patted her on the arm and assured her that everything was fine. She drifted off before she'd counted to ninety, and I began the surgery. I performed a Shirodkar cerclage using a sturdy, braided tape-like suture to envelope the cervix. I then embedded the sutures deep into her cervix and covered the exposed ends of the suture with her vaginal tissue. I finished up, and waited to talk to her after they wheeled her into the recovery room. Everything had gone according to plan.

THE FOLLOWING SUNDAY was a big day for Woody, a chess tournament where he'd have opponents of all ages—children to adults—who were at a similar skill level. He had played a few Pee Wee tournaments previously but those were exclusively against other kids.

It was a lovely, sunny day when we got to Rutherford, about fifteen minutes from our home in Teaneck. The games were being held at a lodge—Rotarians, Knights of Columbus, or something similar. I walked through the entrance with Woody and looked around at the big, old-fashioned, wood-paneled room. Except for the chess sets, it was like being transported into an episode of the television show, *The Honeymooners*. I could almost picture Ralph Kramden and Ed Norton strolling through after attending one of their International Order of Friendly Raccoons meetings.

Everyone was pleasant and welcoming. I wasn't on call and the rest of the weekend stretched out before me. I had brought my needlepoint along to keep me busy as Woody went from match to match.

About halfway through the tournament, my beeper sounded; the answering service was trying to reach me. I found a phone booth, called in, and the service told me to call my patient, Helen Morris.

I got her on the phone a moment later. She was cramping, she said. She was leaking fluid from her vagina. While I couldn't be certain without examining her, it sounded like her membranes had ruptured.

"Go to the hospital," I said, "and I'll meet you there."

I next called Shearwood, told him I had an emergency, and he promised to come down to Woody's tournament. After saying good-bye to my son, who was engrossed in a match with a serious-looking older gentleman, I hurried to the car.

I GOT TO THE hospital in under an hour. Helen had already been admitted. The nurse told me Helen was running a fever of about 102 degrees. That didn't bode well. Add a fever to what she'd told me on the phone and we were probably looking at chorioamnionitis: an infection of the membranes.

That meant I'd have to empty her uterus.

I examined her, confirmed my suspicions, started her on intravenous antibiotics, and told her what we'd have to do. Worst of all from Helen's perspective was that she'd lose yet another baby after getting her hopes up, but she took the news with equanimity. Nurses prepped her for the operating room.

The first order of business, before I could perform a D&C (dilation and curettage), was to take out the sutures I'd just put in a week ago. That wasn't as simple as it might seem. When I'd embedded them in the cervical tissue, I expected them to be in there forever. If I'd done the simpler procedure—the one I expressly decided against to avoid the kind of infection she'd somehow gotten anyway—it would be much easier to undo. Just snip the knot, pull, and out come the stitches. But in the more complex procedure, the cervix is sutured in two layers with the knot covered over. Nothing was visible on the outside.

something to prove

I had to uncover all that before I could do anything else.

As I removed the last of the stitches, her cervix opened. With nothing to hold in the fetus, I immediately saw these two tiny feet hanging out. It was a breech.

At fourteen weeks, Helen's baby was only about four inches long. I completed the delivery, and noticed a little defect of some sort on the fetus' back, probably spina bifida—not that that mattered now.

It was a sad moment but I had to stay focused on making sure that Helen was all right. The placenta followed the fetus out and I was ready to go in and just do a little scrape here and there to make sure everything was clear.

Before I could do that, she started to bleed.

As with my earlier patient, Mary Paulsen, Helen's uterus was refusing to contract back to its tight, normal shape.

The only thing that saves women from bleeding to death in childbirth is that the smooth muscle of the uterus contracts back into its original shape after a baby is delivered; and, in doing so, it clamps all open blood vessels shut. That's nature's sole protection against the extermination of all mothers, everywhere.

If something interferes with nature's design, as was happening with Helen, all those blood vessels remain dilated. And the blood pours out freely.

I started massaging her uterus, tried to smack back the muscle's memory. *Contract, damn it.* Meanwhile, along with the intravenous antibiotics, we pumped in Pitocin and Methergine, two drugs that caused the uterus to contract.

Still she bled. And bled and bled.

Should I pack her with gauze, and try to save her uterus, or forget her baby-making equipment and just concentrate on saving her life? It wasn't a simple question.

If this were a woman with four children at home, I would have gone in and done a hysterectomy without a second thought. But childless Helen wanted a baby. That's why she'd come to me in the first place; she was desperate to become a mother. I didn't want to foreclose that possibility for her forever, not if I could help it.

One factor weighing in favor of trying to preserve her uterus was that she was only fourteen weeks pregnant. It wasn't as if she had been stretched to full-term.

I made my decision. "We're packing her," I said, "Get me some Kerlix." The surgical nurse brought me a roll of the gauze-like material. The idea behind packing the uterus is the same as when dealing with any other wound: you put pressure on it to stop it from bleeding. The Kerlix gauze would exert pressure on all those dilated blood vessels and, with any luck, stanch the flow. I packed her as tightly as I could.

I don't know how many yards of Kerlix I used but the bleeding remitted. Crisis averted—for the moment, at least.

I WAS WRUNG OUT after the effort but I still had more to do. The packing would have to come out the next day or it could exacerbate the infection that had started this problem. But looking at Helen's labs, I worried that once I did remove the packing she might start bleeding again.

I spoke to Helen in the recovery room as she came out of the anesthesia, just to make sure she was all right. Then, I had her transferred from there to the Intensive Care Unit (ICU). Next, I went to Dr. Birnbaum's office to consult on Helen's case.

Dr. Stanley J. Birnbaum was the über-sage of gynecology at Cornell. A tall, bespectacled man with a full head of white hair and an authoritative presence, he had been at New York Hospital for as long as anyone could remember. He had a reputation for being straightforward and good with his hands. In my opinion, Dr. Birnbaum was the best surgeon practicing at the hospital.

Any time I needed a gynecological consult, if he was there, I'd ask Dr. Birnbaum.

I gave him a synopsis of what had occurred to that point. He knew Helen. Everyone did. She was part of our little family in OB-GYN and he was happy to help.

"Let me just come down and look at the whole situation," he said and followed me to the ICU.

I went over Helen's chart and her laboratory values with him. My primary concern was disseminated intravascular coagulopathy or DIC.

DIC is a rare complication but it has the potential to be fatal. It happens when something causes the body to consume all its clotting factors. Without clotting factors, the blood will just pour out of any open cut, the patient will go into shock and, if the physician can't get the situation under control, the patient will die. An infection such as the one that caused Helen's membranes to rupture is a prime candidate for bringing on DIC.

There are blood tests that reflect whether a patient may be going into DIC. Helen's platelets were a little low but the other labs were marginal; she didn't appear to have progressed to that stage. Still, it concerned me.

Dr. Birnbaum reviewed everything and his opinion gave me hope.

"I've been doing this for thirty years, Yvonne, don't worry about it." Birnbaum said, "She's stopped bleeding now. She's borderline, but her blood count isn't getting worse."

He said to take her back to the OR in the morning and remove the packing. And that would be the end of it.

"What if she starts bleeding?" I asked.

"I haven't seen that in years," he answered. Once she's stabilized and she's stopped bleeding, he said, you can remove the packing. Rarely, if ever will they start bleeding again.

His only concern, he said, was that the original infection of her membranes might prevent her uterus from contracting. Infection interferes with the body's ability to react normally in more ways than we can predict. But Dr. Birnbaum's opinion made sense.

With greater optimism and a sense of relief, I returned to Helen's side to tell her what we had discussed and how we were going to proceed.

Helen had lost a lot of blood, and still had a fever. It was not surprising under those circumstances that she seemed out of it, so I kept it simple.

"The worst-case scenario," I said, "is that when I take out the packing you may continue to bleed. I don't expect that to happen because you're stable now. I know you desperately want children, and I'm not even going to think of doing a hysterectomy unless your life depends on it, okay?"

something to prove

She managed a weak, "Okay, Dr. Thornton." I left her side and let her rest.

Helen didn't lose any more blood overnight. Her platelets were still a little low but her blood pressure and her hematocrit were stable. It looked as if the worst was behind us.

IN THE MORNING, we took Helen back to the operating room. Anne Regenstein, one of my residents, diminutive in stature and smart as a whip, was there to assist. This would be the last element of routine care I'd have to complete before Helen could begin to heal. I didn't really need a resident's assistance to remove the packing. I had Annie there because, despite my faith in Dr. Birnbaum's expertise, I wasn't taking any chances. For the same reason, I told an anesthesiologist to stand by outside the OR.

I sat on a stool at the end of the operating table and, with forceps, gingerly started taking out the yards and yards of packing and laying it to the side. It took several minutes to remove it all. It was bloody, but that was to be expected. When I'd packed Helen the day before, she'd been hemorrhaging.

Dr. Birnbaum's advice seemed to have been right.

I swiveled the stool around to get a speculum from the table behind me, so I could take a look inside to make sure everything was okay.

When I swiveled back toward Helen, it was as if a faucet had been turned on inside her, gushing red. Blood poured out of her and dripped all over the floor.

It didn't even look like blood. It was thinner than normal, as if it had been diluted with water. In color and consistency, it resembled nothing so much as wine. Her clotting factors were gone, consumed by the infection that had brought her in the day before. She had progressed to DIC, disseminated intravascular coagulopathy. If I didn't stop the bleeding, and fast, Helen would be dead in minutes.

I called for the anesthesiologist. "You have to put her out, fast. Fast!"

Helen was looking up at me, without understanding. Although a nurse, in her weakened condition, it wasn't clear how much she could grasp of the situation. There was no time to explain. I'd done my explaining in the ICU the previous day.

"Helen, you're hemorrhaging," I said. "We're going to have to go in."

The anesthesia took effect in seconds. Positioned at her abdomen, I made my incision. A normal uterus is a pink color but Helen's was a yellowish-gray, apparently because of the infection. Instead of a tight, contracted muscle, this organ was a flabby sac.

I performed a hysterectomy, but left her ovaries intact. I checked that there were no visible pockets of infection anywhere, and closed her up.

Sweaty and exhausted, I went looking for Helen's next of kin. In the waiting area were her mother and a friend. Taking her mother aside, I sat her down in the doctors' room and told her about the unexpected events we'd confronted, the otherwise unstoppable hemorrhage, and that I'd had no choice but to remove her uterus. It was the only way to keep Helen from bleeding to death. But we *had* saved her.

Her mother didn't acknowledge my comment about pulling Helen back from imminent death.

She looked at me with what appeared to be a mix of anger and disgust.

"Now, no man will want to marry her," she said.

WHEN I GOT HOME that evening, I poured out the day's travails to Shearwood, telling him about the DIC and the hysterectomy. But almost worse than all that was what Helen's mother had said.

"She didn't even ask, 'Is my daughter okay?'"

How could a mother be more concerned about whether a man would now want Helen as his wife than whether she'd survive?

Shearwood, as always, was a stabilizing force, generous with his husbandly support as well as his medical insights.

"Calm down, Yvonne, it's all right," he said, his soft baritone voice an immediate comfort.

Let Helen deal with her mother's skewed priorities. You just saved Helen's life, he reminded me, and should be relieved and happy for that.

HELEN'S TEMPERATURE CONTINUED to spike for the next several days. It would drop to 99, then climb to 102; fall back to 100, then shoot up to 103. Up and down it went like a picket fence.

The chorioamnionitis, the infection of the membranes lining the uterus, should have been gone once her uterus was gone. There had to be some residual infection.

Within days, her incision opened. The wound was filled with purulent material. No wonder Helen's temperature wouldn't stabilize.

I couldn't close the wound, not infected as it was, or I would be closing the bacteria inside, to multiply and spread. It had to heal from the bottom up. I covered the open incision area with dressings and gave instructions to the nurses to change the dressings continually. I adjusted her antibiotics to deal with this new complication, and kept watch.

I put everything non-essential on hold. Shearwood picked up the slack at home so I could be at Helen's bedside, twice a day, seven days a week. And when I wasn't there physically, she was in my thoughts.

I went over every decision, every test, every moment I'd spent on Helen's case, trying to understand what caused the initial chorioamnionitis. I read and re-read her chart, her labs, my notes, looking for clues. Should I have done the less complex cervical procedure? No, I reminded myself, that would have left her even more susceptible to infection. Could the labs have missed signs of infection left over from the one she'd had months before? What could I, should I, have done differently?

The events of the past several days would have weighed on me as a physician no matter who the patient was, but there was a personal element to my concern, too. Helen had worked alongside me. She had been a comrade-in-arms through countless deliveries, some quite difficult. Now, she was on the other side of the table but the connection between us was still strong.

THE FEVERS KEPT COMING, despite the big-gun antibiotics.

After I left Helen to make my rounds, I got a call from one of the nurses that Helen was having trouble breathing. I rushed back to the ICU.

something to prove

She had been asymptomatic, other than the fever, earlier in the day but now, Helen was in obvious distress. Her breathing was labored. She was perspiring. Her temperature had shot up higher and her oxygenation was low.

The most logical cause of this new set of symptoms was a potentially deadly clot in her lungs, an embolism. It may sound crazy that someone who has lost most of her clotting factors could have a clot, but an embolism isn't always comprised of blood. Even though Helen's clotting factors were coming back to normal, there are fat emboli and air emboli, too, and if they travel to the lung they can wreak the same havoc as a blood clot. I ordered oxygen and scheduled a CT scan for that night.

I had no good options. An embolism of any kind that blocks the blood vessels to the lungs can kill very quickly. The blood thinner heparin is the medication of choice to break up an embolism; it's a treatment that can mean the difference between life and death.

But Helen also had DIC, and the last thing you want to give a patient who has lost most of her clotting factors is a medicine that inhibits clotting. If I gave her heparin, she might start bleeding from the open incision wound again. That, too, could kill her.

It was too risky to do more until I knew what I was dealing with.

AT HOME, I TOLD Shearwood my dilemma. As an orthopedic surgeon, Shearwood dealt with his share of emboli, so he was able to do more than comfort. I had an expert to consult with over the dinner table.

"Should I wait to establish the diagnosis," I asked, "or treat empirically?"

"I'd give her the heparin now," he answered. "You can always give her the antidote if she starts to over-anticoagulate. But if you think she has an embolism, don't wait for a diagnosis."

An embolism is so serious, he said, that to delay until I got a definitive answer might mean getting the answer postmortem.

I thanked him, called the ICU, and gave the nurse a verbal order to start Helen on heparin that night.

THE FOLLOWING MORNING I asked for a consultation with a pulmonologist, who looked at Helen's CT scan and recommended another, more specific test to rule out pulmonary embolism.

It turned out not to be an embolism but yet another pocket of infection, this time in her lungs. It was causing an atypical pneumonia, said the pulmonologist, who pronounced her lungs in terrible shape. I stopped the heparin. Again, we changed Helen's antibiotic so it would cover the lung complication as well as the wound infection.

If I were the superstitious sort, I'd have sworn that the woman was jinxed. First, her uterus was infected, then her wound opened, and now she had pneumonia.

She kept spiking temperatures. Within five days of the embolism scare, she complained of pain on urination. I ordered urine cultures. Her urine test showed white blood cells. I called in a nephrologist who found that Helen had a bladder and kidney infection. Once again, we adjusted her antibiotic.

Her case file was now thicker than that of any patient I'd

had previously and I still didn't know what had started her down this path. I again scoured through my notes, the lab reports, and everything else I had, looking for answers that remained elusive. I checked on her twice a day, every day. I brought in infectious disease specialists and any other specialist I could think to consult. Nobody had a definitive answer. Nobody could be sure if Helen would live or die.

We don't think much about fatalities from infections any more, but in earlier times, before the advent of antibiotics, such infection virtually guaranteed a visit from the Grim Reaper. You commonly heard, "Oh, she died in childbirth." If our life expectancy is longer today, it's because we've come so far in combating bacterial disease. But we haven't conquered it completely. Systemic infection with "superbugs" can still evade the weapons we use against it and cause a massive, multisystem shutdown.

Because Dr. Ledger was probably the top expert in the nation on gynecologic infections, I asked him to consult on Helen's case as well.

He suggested checking whether I'd missed a pocket of infection when I first closed her up after the hysterectomy. I did another pelvic exam but found nothing. I sent her for a CT scan and X-ray, but those were negative as well.

THE KIDS HAD BEEN absolute gems throughout this trying time and didn't complain that Mommy was gone more than she was home. It became apparent that my mind was mostly elsewhere, even when I was with them, when Kimmie asked me about her Halloween costume.

"The Halloween costume contest is in just two days, Mommy," she said, very upset. "And I have nothing to wear."

Her third-grade teacher, Miss Amorosi, was going to award a prize to the child who wore the most creative costume and Kimmie had her heart set on winning. "Most creative" didn't mean something we could run to the store to buy. A "most creative" costume required someone applying actual creativity to it.

"What am I supposed to do in two days?" I said.

I didn't remember her telling me about the contest but I couldn't be sure that she hadn't given me all the details while my mind was focused on disseminated intravascular coagulopathy or emboli or the right antibiotic to cover lung and wound and urinary tract infections.

I thought and thought about what Kimmie and I could do in the few hours I had between visits to the hospital. I had taken no days off since Helen had been admitted. If I wasn't on call or teaching or seeing private patients, I still drove in to check on Helen in the ICU, morning and afternoon.

Finally, it came to me. Kimmie had a purple leotard and matching tights. She could go as a bunch of grapes!

I bought several packages of purple balloons, blew them up, and pinned them all over her leotard. Kimmie looked adorable. Best of all, she seemed thrilled with her ad hoc costume. I sent her off to school, and then headed for the hospital. Later that afternoon, she proudly announced that she'd won the prize, even though some kid dressed as Moses tried to pop her balloons.

It was a small victory, but it offered a moment of relief in the midst of a crisis. My daughter needed me and no matter what else was going on, I'd been there for her.

something to prove

HELEN HAD BEEN SCANNED and X-rayed and examined multiple times by a parade of physicians. I couldn't count the number of lab tests I'd ordered, or the list of medications administered. Although I hated putting her through more surgery, the only option left was to open her up again and look with my own eyes. Maybe I'd catch something that way that all the tests missed.

I was on the brink of doing just that when her temperature began to stabilize at about 100 degrees. It wasn't yet normal but it wasn't climbing, either. When I visited her, she said she felt a little better. And each day, she seemed to improve a bit more. About a week later, her temperature had been almost normal for a few days and she was ready to be discharged, still weak, for sure, but alive and on the mend. She had been hospitalized for a full month.

When I watched Helen leave the hospital, it was like seeing Lazarus rise. And it wasn't just me. Among all the specialists who had consulted on her case, there was a collective sense of relief and triumph and gladness. Her survival was a testament both to our skills and the miraculous power of the human body.

THE BODY IS A wonderful thing. If you can fend off the attacks from the hundreds of billions of microbes that conspire to undermine its every organ, if you can determine the right treatments, then the body will take it from there and heal itself.

I still didn't have any answers about the underlying cause of Helen's problems, but knowing she would be well again was better than knowing why she'd become so ill in the first place.

It was a mystery that I would eventually solve but it would take more than a decade to do it.

Can I Still Have a Baby?

ABOUT SIX WEEKS after Helen was discharged from the hospital, she returned to my office for a postoperative checkup. She looked as healthy as if the ordeal had never happened. The only clue left was her incision scar, which itself was healing nicely.

After examining her, I brought her back into my office so we could go over any concerns she might have.

The question she had for me was one I'd never have anticipated.

"Dr. Thornton, can I still have a baby?"

She was an educated nurse, an RN at Cornell. She had to know the answer. But she wasn't thinking clearly. I gently tried to help her come to terms with the situation.

"I had to take out your uterus, Helen. You know what that means."

She looked at me with such intensity. She needed more from me. What else could I say to her?

"You can have a surrogate," I said. "Your ovaries are still there."

I explained that a fertility doctor could take one of her eggs, fertilize it with her boyfriend's sperm, and implant it in a surrogate. While she wouldn't be the one to carry the baby, it would be hers. I hoped that that possibility gave her some comfort.

She said she understood. But long after she left, I thought about the question she'd asked and why she'd asked it. It meant that reality was competing with wishful thinking.

Dr. Thornton and parents Itasker
and Donald Thornton, at her college
graduation in 1969

Dr. Thornton, graduating from
Columbia University's College of
Physicians and Surgeons in 1973

Seated: Dr. Thornton—Chief resident (second left), Dr. Thomas F. Dillon (center)
Standing (1st row) : Dr. Ernst Bartsich (between Dr. Thorton and Dr. Dillon);
Dr. Abraham Risk (behind Dr. Dillon)

Dr. Thornton
interviewed by
The New York Times
about the new
demand for female
obstetricians, 1976
Credit: Tyrone Dukes/
The New York Times/
Redux

Proud granddad Donald
Thornton and grandson
Woody, 1982

Halloween for "Dr." Woody
and Kimberly, 1987

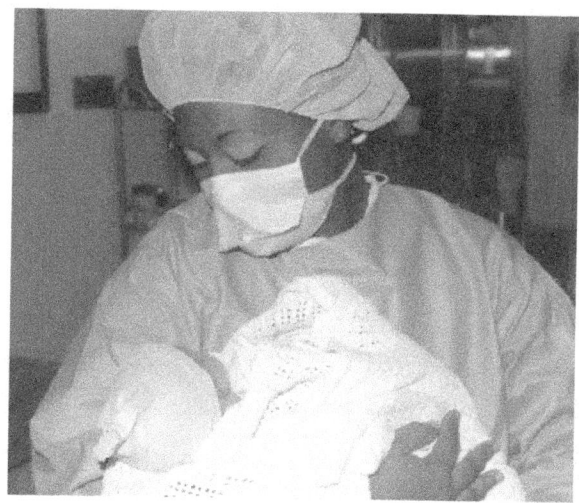

Dr. Thornton with
babe in arms

Dr. Thornton in her office at New York
Hospital-Cornell Medical Center

Kimberly McClelland as a cluster
of grapes, Halloween, 1988

Dr. Thornton as Obstetric Attending of the Month at New York Hospital, 1991
Credit: Courtesy of Medical Center Archives of New York-Presbyterian/Weill Cornell

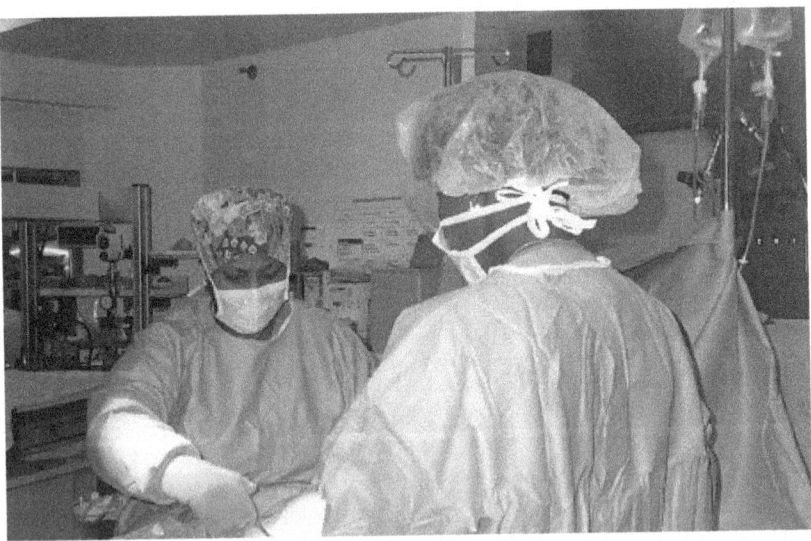

Dr. Thornton performing surgery

chapter eight

Reality: Check

"If you can't get on the other guy's wagon,
you make your own wagon."
—DONALD THORNTON

L IKE ANY OTHER WORKPLACE, New York Hospital–
Cornell Medical buzzed with workplace gossip.

The most recent rumor was that a former resident of mine, Alan Kessler, who had since joined the Cornell faculty as an assistant professor, was about to be promoted to associate professor.

"Did you hear the news?"

"Dr. Kessler is so excited about his promotion."

"Well, he's always been one of Dr. Ledger's favorites."

I nearly fell on the floor. I'd been at Cornell for seven years and had yet to be promoted. I was still an assistant professor. It was actually worse because, not only had I not yet been promoted, Ledger had removed me as the director of the clinic.

something to prove

Dr. Kessler had just finished his residency in 1983. Now, Ledger planned to promote my resident before me? Over my dead body.

Even before I joined the Cornell faculty I was already a double Board-certified maternal-fetal medicine specialist with three years teaching experience at Bethesda. I'd attended one of the most prestigious—and competitive—medical schools in the country, and had completed my residency and fellowship at prestigious and competitive schools.

My former resident, Alan Kessler, had graduated from a medical school in Guadalajara, Mexico. He later transferred to the United States to complete his education.

I liked Kessler. He was an affable fellow who was good with the patients. He'd done well as a resident. But if I had to speculate about why he was being elevated while I was not, I'd guess it was because he had the Cornell boys' club "look"—tall, blond, handsome, and well dressed.

I knew, of course, that there was and always had been a glass ceiling in academic medicine. Women typically got stuck on the bottom rung of the career ladder with the title of assistant professor while the men effortlessly climbed up to associate, then full professor.

Despite my familiarity with the traditional gender favoritism, this felt like an especially low blow.

Seething, I marched into Dr. Ledger's plush, spacious office and told him what we needed to talk about and why.

"Well, you know, Yvonne…" he began.

"No," I said, cutting him off before he could offer his rationale. "I'm double Board-certified. Alan Kessler is a foreign medical graduate from Guadalajara. How is it going to look if he's catapulted over me to become associate professor?"

I reminded him of how hard I'd worked for his department for the past seven years. I should have been an associate professor two years ago—and if I'd looked like Alan Kessler, I would have been.

If Dr. Ledger didn't correct the situation, I told him, I'd leave. And then I played my ace. I'd been building up my private practice at Cornell for all those seven years, I said, and if I left, I'd take those patients with me.

"Yvonne, don't get all excited, we don't have to go there." He said he'd talk to the promotion committee and get back to me.

A few days later, I got a call from Dr. Ledger's secretary. She was starting the process for me to become an associate professor, she said.

On April 1, 1991, New York Hospital–Cornell Medical Center sent out a press release that began with the following:

"The Department of Obstetrics and Gynecology proudly announces the promotion of Dr. Yvonne S. Thornton to Associate Professor of Obstetrics and Gynecology. Dr. Thornton is the first female faculty member to attain this unmodified academic rank in the Department."

I would have preferred that the promotion had come as recognition for my achievements, rather than through an ultimatum, but Daddy had taught me to make my own opportunities. And that's what I'd done.

WOODY'S NEXT CHESS tournament was at a hotel in Somerset, New Jersey, about an hour from home.

something to prove

The games took up several conference rooms on the hotel's second floor. Along the perimeter of the entrances to those meeting rooms was a balcony, giving a view of the lobby below.

Sitting at one of the tables scattered around the balcony, I worked on my needlepoint while Woody played his matches.

He came out to talk to me between games, telling me how he'd made this move or that, captured this piece or had that one captured. He might as well have been speaking Mandarin for all I understood, but it was nice to hear the excitement in my son's voice.

Kids were scooting back and forth along the balcony area between the tables and conference rooms, the older kids well-behaved, the younger ones less so. As Woody spoke to me about his last match, another boy passed us. I vaguely noticed him in my peripheral vision but Woody stopped talking, mid-sentence, and just gawked.

"I've got to get me one of those," he said. "I'm *going* to get me one of those."

"One of what?" I asked.

He kept staring across my shoulder.

I turned to see what had caught his attention. It was the boy's red jacket. It didn't look like anything special, just the usual sort of windbreaker that you see with the logo of a sports team. On the back of this one, which Woody could see from where he was sitting but I hadn't noticed until I turned around, was embroidered in big white letters, "All-America Chess Team."

He looked longingly at the thing, craning his neck as the kid in the jacket turned the corner.

Reality: Check

WOODY ASKED AROUND at his chess matches what it would take to become a member of the All-America Chess Team, and discovered that among about 28,000 kids competing for the honor, fewer than fifty are selected. The odds against him were enormous.

It didn't deter him.

He asked his chess teacher, Mr. Friedman, to give him more homework. He immersed himself in a set of books called *Chess Informant,* studying the openings, middle games, and end games that the multiple volumes detailed in something called "chess notation." It looked like total gobbledygook to me, but Woody committed it all to memory. I'd never seen him so driven.

He didn't just *want* to be a member of the All-America Chess Team, with an All-America Chess Team jacket. He *needed* it. He was as committed as any fairy-tale knight on his way to slay a dragon. It was his quest.

And so, when he did poorly at his first New Jersey Scholastic Tournament, it felt like a major defeat. He lost the first two games and came out of his last match in tears. He was just inconsolable.

I have always felt my children's pain more acutely than my own. I couldn't handle seeing Woody so distraught, especially when I could do nothing to make him feel better. I didn't even understand when he tried to explain what had gone wrong, something about where he should have moved his pawn, I think, or maybe it was the bishop. Not that it would have made much difference if I'd known which piece, in retrospect, he believed he'd moved to the wrong square.

something to prove

How can you help when your child is expressing himself in what, for all intents and purposes, is a foreign language to you?

When we got home, I told Shearwood that from then on he'd have to accompany Woody to his chess tournaments. I couldn't bear to watch my baby cry.

Shearwood, always my rock, readily agreed.

Pretty soon, Kimmie began going to the tournaments with her brother and Dad. Mr. Friedman said that Kimmie was unusually talented too, but she wasn't obsessed. For her it was still a game, not a calling.

Anytime she got cornered in a difficult match, instead of trying to figure a way out of her predicament, she would say, "I'm tired now, you can win."

It was getting close to Halloween again and Kimmie wanted to wear a Tina Turner costume to school. When I heard that, I put my foot down.

"Tina Turner?" I said. "You are not going to be that wild woman with the earrings and the short-short miniskirt. Oh no, not my daughter, absolutely not."

She begged, but I wouldn't have it. I would *not* permit my child to strut around in a skimpy outfit. She could be a princess, I said. And that was the end of it.

A couple days later, they had a chess tournament at the Manhattan Chess Club. Shearwood took the kids and I stayed home, but Shearwood called me with a progress report.

You have to win the most out of five games to win the tournament, and each game gets progressively more difficult. Woody was doing quite well but Kimmie had lost her first two.

I knew she could have won at least one. She wasn't even trying.

"Put her on the phone," I said, remembering how Daddy would give me and my sisters incentives to do our best when we were little.

"You want to be Tina Turner?" I asked when she came on the line. "You win the next three games, you can be Tina Turner."

Now, I admit, I knew full well that she didn't have a prayer. If she couldn't win the first two games of the tournament, she wasn't going to win all three of the more difficult remaining ones. But I wanted her to at least try. When Shearwood got back on the line, I explained all this.

Shearwood agreed that it was smart to at least give her something to strive for.

I didn't give it another thought until a few hours later, when Shearwood called back.

"Kimmie won!" he told me. He had difficulty believing it himself, but he saw it with his own eyes. Not only had she aced her next three games, she had beaten a player who was rated so many points above her that she might as well have been matched with Bobby Fischer.

While I was happy that she'd applied herself and won, I was considerably less happy that I had to follow through on my promise.

I got the costume for her: too-short leather miniskirt, matching leather jacket, spiky blonde wig, and outlandishly dangling faux-tusk earrings.

It wasn't bad enough that she wore that costume to school. That day, Kimmie's class went to Holy Name Hospital to show off their costumes to the little sick kids. I could only hope that none of the doctors at Holy Name realized that the child dressed up as a wild woman was the daughter of Dr. Thornton and Dr. McClelland.

But now I knew that my little girl could be just as focused as my little boy. It all depended on how much each of them wanted something.

Woody, of course, still wanted that jacket. With every match, he kept score of how close he was getting.

Those who made the All-America Chess Team had to win a certain number of rated tournaments, and a certain number of games within a tournament. Every time he lost, he'd say, "Okay, that's two points down, I've got to get three points."

In his *Chess Informant* books, he went over the matches played between world-famous chess masters that were laid out move-by-move in each volume. These were the same books that helped Garry Kasparov and Anatoly Karpov become world champions and Woody seemed determined to follow in their path. He studied the books whenever he had a free moment. I even caught him sneaking peeks at a *Chess Informant* during Thanksgiving dinner. He had it stowed underneath his chair. He was going to get himself one of those jackets, no matter what the odds.

His determination was starting to pay off. Woody won his first tournament: he was now the New Jersey Junior State Champion. There was no stopping him now.

Even though Woody, my little chess champion, no longer had anything to cry about, having Shearwood take over chess duty was a relief for me. While he, too, rotated on call for emergencies, there is no orthopedic equivalent to, "Doctor, my water broke." Shearwood could have his attending take charge until he arrived. His surgeries were almost always laid out nicely and neatly in his appointment book.

Mine, too often, were the result of urgent calls. One of my mentors once told me that the practice of obstetrics can be defined as many, many hours of sheer boredom interrupted by a few minutes of total chaos. "Total chaos" almost seemed too tame a description for my afternoon call that next Saturday.

I WAS COVERING NIGHTS and weekends in rotation with another perinatologist, and got a call from the hospital that I was needed in what appeared to be an emergency situation. A woman had come in, on transfer from another hospital. She was twenty-eight weeks pregnant and had not seen a doctor since her pregnancy began. She probably thought she'd just show up at the hospital when labor started but now, at the beginning of her third trimester, she was in pain and realized she needed help.

The resident who examined her asked for a maternal-fetal medicine specialist's evaluation because something just didn't look right. Or, more to the point, he said that something didn't feel right when he palpated her abdomen.

"It's just strange, Dr. Thornton," was all the advance warning I got from the resident.

"Strange" turned out to be an understatement.

I entered the exam room, introduced myself, and did my own examination. I could swear I felt a leg, knee, and thigh, right there under my fingers. I could actually feel the baby's kneecap. I shouldn't have been able to feel any of that, not if the baby was enclosed in the uterus. All the fetus' extremities were moving just beneath this patient's skin.

Not wanting to alarm the patient. I simply told her that we needed to monitor her and that she was going to be taken upstairs to Labor and Delivery. Because she'd had two previous cesarean deliveries and was now in persistent pain, we would be delivering this baby by cesarean.

As the woman was taken to the eighth floor, I huddled with the attending obstetrician and two residents, and told them what I thought.

"It looks like an ectopic pregnancy."

"Wouldn't that rupture the tube?" asked one of the residents.

I explained that this pregnancy wasn't in the fallopian tube. If it had been, it would indeed have ruptured and the patient would be dead by now. But there are different types of ectopic pregnancies. Ovarian and cervical pregnancies are also possible and would also have caused hemorrhaging long before this point. This baby was twenty-eight weeks along. It had to have grown outside of the uterus to begin with, and the only possibility, I said, was an abdominal pregnancy. Granted, I had never seen an abdominal pregnancy before, although I'd read of such cases in my pathology books. Everything pointed to the likelihood that I'd gotten my first such case in the flesh.

"But how does it get there?" asked a resident.

Good question. For a short time, I explained, as the egg is released from the ovary during ovulation, it's actually in the abdomen. There are little thread-like projections called fimbria in the fallopian tubes, and they're supposed to sweep the egg from the ovary into the tube, much like a vacuum cleaner. Then, when the sperm comes up the cervix, like a heat-seeking missile, it finds and fertilizes the egg in the tube. A few days later, the fertilized egg rolls down the remaining length of the tube and settles quite nicely into the plush lining of the uterus.

But in some extremely rare cases, the sperm catches up with the egg in that tiny moment while it is still in the abdominal cavity, before the little thread-like fimbria have the chance to sweep the egg where it's supposed to go. Or the pregnancy might actually have been an early ectopic pregnancy in the tube that aborted into the abdominal cavity and started growing. However it gets there, the fertilized egg just hangs out somewhere in the abdomen, develops a placenta, and attaches itself to the bladder or the intestine, sucking the blood and oxygen and nutrients from that organ in order to develop.

If it attaches to the intestine, the woman usually dies, because the placenta will puncture the bowel and cause massive infection as fecal material leaks into the abdomen.

So far, though, other than her complaints about pain, our lady seemed fine. If I was right about this ectopic pregnancy, it was going to be one hell of a job keeping her that way. We had to go in and hope to God.

We got the patient into the OR and I made my incision to perform the cesarean. Sure enough, there was the fetus, fully formed, right on the bowel. I carefully delivered the tiny baby girl. She couldn't have weighed more than two pounds, but she seemed perfectly healthy. That was the easy part. I handed her off to the neonatologist, who took the baby to the neonatal ICU while I turned back to the more serious problem. I had this large placenta hanging off the intestine. If I tried to peel it away, I could rupture the blood vessels of the bowel supplying the placenta and cause sudden and massive hemorrhaging. If I didn't, the mother would probably have equally big problems including infection, abscess formation, adhesions, and bowel obstruction.

Despite my many years of training and experience with difficult pregnancies, the kind of surgery this patient needed was outside my realm of expertise.

There was only one surgeon I knew whom I could imagine dealing with the nightmare mingling of intestine and placenta before me. Daniel Smith was a gynecological oncologist, triple Board-certified, and just the best surgeon possible for what confronted me on that operating table.

Gynecological oncologists are OB-GYNs who have done extra training in cancer surgery, so they really know all the intricacies of the bowel. I told my assistant to get an urgent page out to Dr. Smith and told the anesthesiologist to keep the patient anesthetized. I remained masked and gowned, and waited. And waited. I covered the open incision with a sterile moist cloth, paced around the operating room, and hoped that Dan Smith would arrive shortly.

It was probably only minutes later but it felt like an eternity until he called back.

I heard his voice on the line and said, "Dan, you've got to come up here. Quick."

I explained the situation as briefly as I could. He was in a little bistro on East 72nd Street, enjoying a cool one, but he dropped what he was doing and ran. Within fifteen minutes of my call, he was there. One look at him—he was wearing these funny little khaki-colored Bermuda shorts—and I could see that he'd been anticipating a leisurely Saturday. No chance of that now. He scrubbed, suited up, and got ready to go.

All I could say was, "Thank God you're here."

"I haven't seen one of these in many years," he said as he looked at the patient on the table.

I let Smith take over and acted as his first assistant as he worked slowly and painstakingly, reviewing every inch of intestine to see where the placenta adhered and where the vessels could be tied and cut, releasing parts of the placenta from its implantation site. The placenta's tentacle-like appendages, called trophoblasts, had latched on tightly across a wide section of the bowel, tapping into the rich blood supply of the gut to feed the baby who had grown there.

"If I remove most of the placenta, we'll have to do a bowel resection," he said, referring to surgery that involves cutting away part of the intestine. Doing that would mean that the woman would be stuck with a colostomy bag, something we wanted to avoid if at all possible.

There was still a danger of damaging the delicate internal organs, even without removing the entire placenta. Dan excised what he could. Hours later, he had only been able to safely remove about one-quarter of the placenta's tissue; he clamped off the rest.

We gave her a medication called methotrexate that shrinks the placenta over a period of weeks, and crossed our fingers.

We monitored her for six months, watching for any delayed complications. But she was fine. Her baby was fine. That the mother came out of this with nothing more than a cesarean scar was a minor miracle.

THE OB-GYN DEPARTMENT was abuzz with gossip again. Dr. Druzin, according to the rumors, would be moving back to California the following year, to join the faculty at Stanford. I'd known that he was unhappy in New York and had wanted to go back to the West Coast. Everyone knew. I wondered if, perhaps, this meant I'd misunderstood Dr. Ledger's intentions when he removed me as director of the clinic. Could Dr. Ledger have taken the clinic directorship from me because he realized he'd need me to step into Dr. Druzin's position? No matter what Ledger felt toward me personally, he had a department to run. And I was next in line, the only perinatologist whose qualifications matched Druzin's. While all the physicians at Cornell were exceptional in their own ways, Druzin and I had been Board-certified in maternal-fetal medicine the same year, had equivalent experience both on faculty and in clinical practice. No other perinatologist on Cornell's staff matched either my credentials or my experience. Of course, Ledger could have been planning to bring in a director from a different institution. But if so, the rumor mill would have been buzzing about that, too. And on the subject of a new director, the mill was silent.

Dr. Ledger hadn't said anything to me but, until Druzin made his departure official, I didn't expect him to.

Although I didn't want to get my hopes up, I'd seen Ledger's practical side. He had backed me up when I laid down the law to voluntary staff and revoked their operating room privileges when they failed to show up to supervise the residents. And he put me in charge of the chorionic villus sampling research. Since FDA approval of the device, that decision had paid off handsomely for Cornell. Counting on Dr. Ledger's pragmatism to override any antipathy he felt toward me, I was more optimistic about my future at Cornell than I had been in years.

Meanwhile, Steve Klein, a Long Island perinatologist in private practice whom I'd met at a perinatal retreat in Vail, Colorado, about a dozen years earlier, when we were both fellows, had been trying to talk me into opening a New Jersey office as his partner. He'd pointed out how nice it would be to have my nights and weekends to myself, to never be on call. He kept saying, "Just think about it, Yvonne. No night call." His practice was a freestanding perinatal center involved only in fetal surveillance and testing, not deliveries and, if I joined him, that's all I'd do. I'd interpret the results of ultrasound and other prenatal tests, and consult with the patients' obstetricians. He said that I could pick out the space and he and his partner would set it up. They'd finance everything. They had the money. They just needed the doctor and the expertise.

I had to admit, it was a great idea. Until the 1980s, any sort of major testing that a patient might need done was typically done in a hospital. But this was the beginning of the nineties and we were seeing more ambulatory surgery. There was no reason why ultrasound or most other prenatal testing had to be done inside a hospital. It would be less expensive for the patient and more lucrative for the doctor to move testing from a hospital setting to a freestanding private facility.

"We could have this on the outside," he said, "and you'd be making much more money than you're making now."

something to prove

"Steve, it's never been about the money for me," I said. "It's about teaching residents."

So, become an adjunct faculty at another medical school, he said, and teach once a week.

To complete his pitch, Dr. Klein pointed out, rather bluntly, that I wasn't likely to get ahead at Cornell. I'd never be anything other than just another worker bee.

"This is an opportunity to be your own person," he said.

I told him thanks, but I was happy at Cornell.

"Think about it," he insisted.

I told him I would, but I'd already made up my mind.

Not interested.

A FEW MONTHS LATER, a younger colleague, Frank Chervenak, dropped in to see me at my sub-basement office. Frank was one of the nicest physicians at Cornell, a chubby-cheeked guy whose dark hair was getting a little thin on top. He'd joined the faculty in 1987 and was also Board-certified in maternal-fetal medicine. But he focused on obstetrical ethics and ultrasound, and didn't get involved in the management of patients. Ultrasound, the hot new thing in prenatal testing, was also the focus of the perinatal center that Steve Klein operated in Long Island.

None of the other faculty showed up in the sub-basement except for clinic duty. After a bit of small talk, my curiosity got the better of me and I had to ask:

"What brings you down here, Frank?"

He mentioned something about hoping that I'd be happy for him. And then, the bomb dropped.

"I've just been named the new Director of Maternal-Fetal Medicine," he said.

Ledger gave him my promotion?

I don't know what Frank expected me to say or do, but he couldn't have anticipated my reaction. Nor could I.

Despite my vow to follow my father's advice never to let others know when they've upset me, I lost it. I just couldn't stop myself. Emotional overload. I began weeping uncontrollably.

"Oh, my God, did I say something?" Frank asked. "What did I do? Did I say something wrong?"

I know that he gave me his handkerchief, and between sobs I could hear him asking why I was crying, but I suddenly felt all alone in that room and a million miles away.

Why was I crying? What could I say? I got myself under control enough to give him the only answer I could.

"It should have been me, Frank. It should have been me."

I hated Ledger at that moment. The bastard didn't have the balls to tell me himself. Ledger must have told Frank that if he wanted this plum position, he'd have to come talk to me about it.

But Frank was such a sweetheart and I wanted to feel happy for him, I truly did. All I could feel though, was hurt.

It should have been me.

And, if there were some reason why Dr. Ledger thought Frank Chervenak, who was a renowned ultrasound expert, but rarely if ever involved himself in delivering babies, should supervise the management and delivery of all high-risk pregnancies at New York Hospital, then Ledger should have been man enough to explain why. To my face.

something to prove

I thought of how foolish I had been to tell Steve Klein I was happy at New York Hospital–Cornell. Steve had been right. I'd never be anything but a worker bee in Ledger's eyes.

This is an opportunity to be your own person, Steve had said. I hadn't been ready to listen at the time.

But now? I was all ears.

I signed a contract committing to a joint venture with Steve Klein and his partner, Ira Spector. I wasn't going to give up my position at Cornell—not yet, anyway—but I was going to start thinking of my future beyond the New York Lying-In Hospital.

I planned to extricate myself once the private practice was well established; and in the meantime I got assurances from Ledger that as long as the private venture didn't interfere with my duties to Cornell, he had no problem with my pursuing it.

I was soon in for another unpleasant surprise. A process server showed up at my office with a subpoena. Helen Morris, the woman whose life I had saved after she developed a massive systemic infection, was suing me for malpractice.

In order for Helen's case to proceed to trial, another doctor would have to swear that my care of Helen Morris was below standard. Apparently, Helen had found such a doctor, right before the statute of limitations was to expire. The attorney for the hospital told me that my file on Helen was the most thorough and comprehensive he'd ever seen—and written in calligraphy, no less (I'd learned calligraphy from an aunt when I was a girl and had written in it since).

He didn't see how any physician would be able to swear that I, or any other physician at Cornell, for that matter, had been less than heroic in our efforts on Helen's behalf.

I had never been accused of malpractice before, thank God. I realized that plenty of good doctors get sued, but to have someone who I'd worked beside and cared about bring a lawsuit against me felt like a knife through the heart. I couldn't imagine what led Helen to this decision. Was it due to despair at losing the ability to have children? Was she not thinking clearly yet (as she hadn't been when, after her hysterectomy, she asked whether she could still get pregnant)? Was it simply a matter of money?

I tried to imagine what Daddy would say to all this. He'd tell me to get on with my life, just keep going, no matter what the setbacks. So, to the extent that I could, I put it out of my mind and focused, instead, on finding a place to open the New Jersey office of the Madonna Perinatal Services, my joint venture with Steve Klein.

THANK GOD FOR MY family. Shearwood and the kids were the better part of my world and they sustained me through the setbacks in my professional life. But now, my eleven-year-old little girl was getting curious about boys. I knew it was time for the birds-and-bees talk but had been waiting for the right moment.

One day, when I got a call to come to the hospital because one of my patients was in labor, Kimmie surprised me.

"Can I come?" she asked.

Sure, I told her. She'd never been interested before. This might be the perfect opportunity to have that talk.

My patient thought it was the cutest thing that I'd brought my daughter along.

So Kimberly watched me as I examined my patient. She shadowed me as I encouraged the soon-to-be new mother through about twelve hours of labor pains. I explained every detail to my daughter as it was happening.

This is the result, I said, after men and women get together and the woman is with child.

Kimberly saw it all and seemed completely fascinated.

I'd expected to show my daughter a routine delivery, but babies have a habit of springing surprises. This one was going to be too big for a vaginal delivery.

It would be necessary to perform a cesarean.

It was about 11:00 at night. I asked Kimberly if she wanted her father to come pick her up, but she said no. She wanted to stay and watch.

At that time, New York Hospital–Cornell Medical Center still had the old galleries overlooking the operating theater, so I walked up the stairs with Kimmie and sat her down in the gallery.

"Honey, you stay up here," I said. "You can look down and see Mommy."

I asked the nurses to check on her every so often, and then I went down into the operating theater to do the cesarean. About halfway through the surgery, I asked one of the nurses how Kimberly was doing and the nurse assured me that my daughter was fine. After a while, I actually forgot Kimberly was there, because my whole focus had to be on my patient.

The delivery went well. I closed up the incision and then went upstairs to ask my daughter if she had been excited to see new life come into the world.

I could tell immediately that "excited" wasn't exactly the word she had in mind.

"That baby and all that tissue, too?" she said. "Never in my wildest dreams did I ever think that it was going to be like this, Mommy."

She was totally turned off.

That was the first and last time we talked about the birds and the bees. I had a feeling that the night's show-and-tell would do more to convince her not to let herself get pregnant than any amount of lecturing.

I FOUND AN OFFICE in Bergen County, New Jersey, for the new branch of Madonna Perinatal Services. I was then introduced to one of the best perinatal ultrasound technicians in New York City, Cheryl Rosen; and an awesome Master's-prepared perinatal nurse specialist, Carol Ruf, graduate of Columbia University School of Nursing and the quintessential perinatal nurse practitioner. With our outstanding perinatal staff and the latest in equipment, I had little doubt we would be a hit. Local obstetricians just needed to know we were there.

But Shearwood said he had a bad feeling about the whole deal. Nothing I could say could change his mind.

I took Shearwood's concerns to heart but I still felt I had to take the chance.

After many unexpected delays in trying to get the Center up and running, we finally opened for business after the High Holy Days in October, 1991. I worked at Cornell during the day and spent nights and weekends at the new office. Much of the time, I had nothing to do. The promised marketing campaign had yet to happen, so very few Bergen County doctors knew about Madonna Perinatal Services. With the country deep in recession, the Long Island office had been losing money and couldn't afford to follow through on the original plan.

Steve Klein and Ira Spector asked me to chip in until the venture got off the ground, which I was happy to do. I handed over the balance of what I'd gotten from the bank loan I had secured for my new corporation, and added much more from my own savings.

Then, one afternoon in December, while I was at Cornell, I got a call from Carol Ruf.

Klein and Spector had sent a truck to the Bergen County office of Madonna Perinatal Services. Without a word of warning, just two months after we opened, they were hauling away all the leased equipment to the Long Island office and closing down the office in New Jersey. They backed up the truck, cleaned out the Center, and went back to Long Island.

Shearwood, unfortunately, had been right, as usual. It was not just the end of my joint venture; it was the last I would see of my money.

DISAPPOINTED AS I WAS, I turned my attention back to fulfilling Mommy's dream of getting a book written about our family.

We had moved our Thornton Sisters' reunions away from the park at Lakewood a year or two earlier. Now, each of us took turns hosting our get-togethers at our homes. The previous summer, it had been my turn. I'd hired a DJ who set up in the gazebo. My sisters brought their instruments and it was like old times again. We had a blast playing tunes like "Respect," some old Supremes' songs, and "Knock On Wood."

The Christmas holiday get-together was promising to be more sedate. It was Jeanette's turn to host and she decided to have us meet at the restaurant in the Plaza Hotel in New York City. Shearwood and I had spent our first night as husband and wife at The Plaza Hotel. The Plaza is the epitome of luxury in a city known for luxury. Modeled after a French Renaissance chateau, the landmark near the southern edge of Central Park attracted well-heeled visitors from around the world. I was surprised that Jeanette had opted to be so extravagant, but it was her year and I didn't feel it was my place to question her choice.

I did have my own contribution to bring to the table: a potential author for a book about our family. His name was Phil Galdston, a songwriter who was making his mark and who had seen both the *Reader's Digest* and *New York Times* articles about our family. He found our story inspiring, and had both a book and a TV mini-series in mind.

I'd sensed some tension from my sisters after the *Reader's Digest* article ran and I thought that getting them involved from the beginning would be a good way to gain their support—and that the family reunion would be the perfect time to introduce them to Phil Galdston. I warned Galdston that Jeanette might not be so welcoming, but he was game.

We agreed to meet in a small conference room at the Plaza a couple of hours before dinner.

My first shock came when I saw my oldest sister, Donna, for the first time in several months. I knew that the lupus had been attacking her lungs. Her rheumatologist had warned me, years earlier. But I wasn't emotionally prepared to see her confined to a wheelchair, her breathing assisted by an oxygen tank.

I didn't have much time to focus on her weakened condition, though, because Rita and Jeanette almost immediately began tearing into Phil Galdston.

He'd brought a synopsis of our story that he wanted my sisters to read. It was based partly on the articles he'd read and partly on interviews he'd done with me. I thought it captured our family's lives well. Donna and Linda gave no indication of how they felt. But Jeanette and Rita were quick with their reactions.

"How dare you presume to write about our family?"

"It's all about Yvonne; what about me?"

"What gives you the right...?"

I was so embarrassed that I zoned out, unable to follow which of the two was hurling which insult. Jeanette and Rita verbally battered the poor writer for the next several minutes, the first sister picking up the insults and acrimony where the last one left off.

He sat there quietly as they harangued him, this kind, mild-mannered man, looking more and more like a whipped puppy.

At last, he got up, said, "Good night, ladies. It's been nice meeting you," and backed out of the room.

I followed him out, and apologized profusely. He insisted there was no need, but he was simply being polite.

"I don't think they're ready," he said, "and if I don't have everybody's permission, I don't feel comfortable going forward."

Mommy and Daddy had always taught us to be polite in front of strangers and to settle our differences among ourselves in private. Well, Jeanette and Rita had thrown that lesson right out the window.

I wasn't going to give up on the book though. Hearing from Phil Galdston had gotten me excited about the idea that had been on the back burner for years, and I needed something positive in my life after so many setbacks. I'd keep looking for a writer but I knew not to make the same mistake again. I wouldn't have the next writer talk to my sisters. My siblings would get copies once the book was published.

chapter nine

May the Future Be as Kind and Honest to You...

"Keep a fresh horse in the barn well-fed and ready to go, because the horse you are riding on now may come up lame."

—DONALD THORNTON

A FEW MONTHS BEFORE Dr. Druzin was scheduled to depart Cornell for Stanford, I got a brochure in the mail from the American College of Obstetricians and Gynecologists about a conference on high-risk pregnancies. It was being held in Maui, Hawaii.

And Cornell's OB-GYN Department was the conference sponsor.

Almost everyone who had a practice at Cornell involving high-risk pregnancy was on the program: Druzin, Ledger,

Chervenak, and several other physicians from the department. In addition, Dr. Ledger had apparently asked non-Cornell physicians to present at the conference as guest faculty.

The brochure listed a veritable who's who of Cornell's maternal-fetal medicine specialists with one glaring exception: nowhere was there any mention of my name. But then, nobody—not Ledger, not Druzin, not anyone else at Cornell—had even told me there *was* a conference.

I could have barged into Ledger's office and complained about being left out. I was one of the two most senior perinatologists on faculty, and the other one was quitting to join the faculty at another medical school. But I knew whatever protests I made would only be ignored and summarily dismissed. I'd grown accustomed to being marginalized and excluded. I couldn't even claim to be surprised that they'd kept me in the dark.

I told myself not to think of it. I had kids to worry about. I had patients to care for. I convinced myself I wasn't all that hurt by the snub.

But Maui would have been nice.

A FEW WEEKS LATER, I was taking the elevator upstairs, standing in the left corner toward the front, surrounded by a number of other people, including Morrie Druzin. An administrator, Colette Carmeris, was in the right corner, toward the back, across from Druzin.

"Oh, Morrie," said Colette, "What's happening with the course in Hawaii?"

Druzin quickly put his fingers to his lips, apparently unaware that I could see him in my peripheral vision.

"Shhh," was all he said. Did he think I couldn't hear him, either?

Colette glanced at me and clammed up.

I pretended not to notice any of this; the doors opened and I exited.

It wasn't until the schedule was made up for the month of April that someone finally mentioned the conference to me. I was going to have to be on call for the weekend because everybody else would be in Hawaii.

DR. MAURICE DRUZIN LEFT New York Hospital for Stanford later that year and I had not a single fond memory of him after almost a decade of working in the same department. Frank Chervenak took over as the new Director of Maternal-Fetal Medicine and, other than the pain of being passed over for the promotion, I didn't realize at first that I would be affected. But I was, profoundly.

Dr. Ledger had promoted to director a physician who was superb at ultrasound. He was also highly respected as an ethicist. But those skills were of no help in the operating room when a woman needed an emergency cesarean. Frank wasn't the type of specialist you'd call upon when a mother was hemorrhaging after giving birth. A resident wouldn't turn to him for guidance about managing a patient who had severe preeclampsia or one who required a difficult forceps delivery.

Yet all such high-risk obstetrics cases fell under maternalfetal medicine, the department Dr. Chervenak now directed.

Because I had a private practice at Cornell and was the most senior maternal-fetal medicine specialist actively practicing, in any and all high-risk pregnancies—whether for a quick consultation or assistance in an emergency—I became the go-to physician.

Residents, fellows, and attendings would call down to my sub-basement office with their urgent requests, interrupting my appointments.

And I'd have to tell my secretary, Mrs. Kiman, to shuffle my patients and put everyone on hold while I dashed up to labor and delivery or over to the clinic on the other side of the sub-basement.

I may not have gotten the title of Director of Maternal-Fetal Medicine but I had the workload. I didn't mind. I loved my work. This was what I was meant to do.

My family was, as always, understanding when this or that emergency kept me from getting home in time for dinner, but the private practice nurses expected to leave the office at 5:00 p.m. I wasn't able to squeeze in all my patients *and* all the emergencies, though, unless I worked late.

The nurses complained of the late hours to the departmental administrator, Leslie McKenzie, and Ms. McKenzie complained to me.

I couldn't ignore the emergencies and I couldn't expect the residents to go to Frank, whose subspecialties within a sub-specialty had little to do with the urgent situations that arise while delivering babies. The only option that made sense was to cut back on my private practice. I told Mrs. Kiman to decrease the number of appointments she scheduled, so that I'd have time to help when I was called and still keep the nurses happy.

With my time freed up to consult where and when I was needed, I figured, problem solved. I didn't think more about it until one morning in January 1992, before my first patient appointment, I got a visit from Ms. McKenzie.

She walked in through my private entrance, the one that bypasses the waiting room, so not even Mrs. Kiman knew she was coming. Leslie McKenzie was a tall, slender no-nonsense type with a face so ordinary it was immediately forgettable. She wore her brown hair in a short ducktail do, and favored business suits that were as nondescript as her features. She was not prone to small talk. Only rarely did I have any reason to speak to her, although she'd recently conveyed the complaints from the nurses about long hours. Her dominion was the OB-GYN Department, near Dr. Ledger's office, and I couldn't imagine what had brought her to the sub-basement.

"We need to talk about your receipts," she said, with no preamble. Compared to the previous year, she said, my faculty private practice revenue was down. As a result, I was in deficit, according to Ms. McKenzie, and I needed to start bringing in more money. Otherwise, she warned, my supplementary compensation—in other words, the lion's share of my salary—would be reduced.

Even after decreasing the number of private practice appointments, I still brought tens of thousands of dollars per month into Cornell. My faculty practice compensation was a mere fraction of that. How could I be in deficit?

For several months I'd been trying to get Ms. McKenzie to explain the strange charges that appeared on the "Faculty Practice Plan Financial Statement" she sent me. Every possible penny got charged against the practice, from billing, administrative costs, employee fringe benefits, nurses' salaries, and rent of my sub-basement office, right down to the last urine sample dipstick and paper clip. But there were several vaguely named charges on the financial statement, too, that McKenzie refused to explain, including more than eight thousand dollars for "Department Clinical Charges," almost two thousand dollars for "Faculty Practice Plan Institutional Development," another two thousand dollars for "Departmental Development Charges," and—the strangest item on the list—sixteen hundred dollars per month for "Indirect Cost." Add it all up and the mystery charges totaled more than double what the hospital paid me in salary for my faculty practice.

And what the heck was "Indirect Cost," anyway?

Each time I'd asked McKenzie to explain all those nebulously worded expenses, she'd brushed me off.

"You don't need to worry about that," she'd answered. "That's the department's concern." Ms. McKenzie was Dr. Ledger's surrogate in these matters, so (reading between the lines) I figured Ledger didn't want me to know.

Because I was on salary, the costs didn't appear to be coming out of my pocket. But now, I realized, if those phantom charges had helped push my receipts into deficit, the charges *were* coming out of my pocket after all. A while back, I'd also learned—from a physician who had closed his Cornell faculty private practice and opened his own Park Avenue office—what some of those mysterious charges paid for. Receipts from the more successful, established practices, like mine, were used to subsidize the junior faculty practices. New faculty needed secretaries, malpractice insurance, and everything else, but they didn't bring in enough money, at first, to pay for it all. Even learning that, I'd never minded—until this moment. It's one thing for the hospital to take money out of my receipts to support the junior faculty; it's quite another to take the money my patients paid to be delivered or treated by me, deduct a huge chunk to pay the junior faculty, and then claim there wasn't enough left over to pay my full salary, too.

Because I wasn't supposed to know anything about all those fuzzy financial statement line items, I played dumb and simply told Ms. McKenzie that she was putting me in a Catch-22 situation.

"You have residents coming to me for help and nurses complaining to you when they have to stay late," I said. I could either cut back on the number of patients Mrs. Kiman scheduled, which would get the nurses out the door at 5:00 p.m.; or I could see more patients and increase the receipts, and the nurses would have to stay later. I couldn't satisfy both demands.

She glared at me without responding.

After our impromptu meeting ended and I began seeing my patients for the day, I stopped by Mrs. Kiman's desk and told her to fill up my schedule again. I knew that the next time there was a breech birth, and I had to run to help, I'd get behind and the nurses would be up in arms again. The nurses would have to sort it out with McKenzie and Ledger. It was out of my hands.

Just to have a record of everything, I wrote to Dr. Ledger, recapping the discussion with Leslie McKenzie. I said that after increasing my patient load, if my receipts were still "in deficit," I'd agree to have my salary cut ... but only if he gave me documentation that every other physician in the department whose receipts were in deficit *also* took a salary cut.

I knew that even with a reduced patient load, my faculty private practice, which had been thriving for ten years, brought in at least as much money to Cornell as almost anyone else's. I was helping to finance physicians who couldn't yet carry their own weight, including some of Ledger's favorites. So, unless Ledger was planning to reduce almost all the other faculty salaries in the department, he would be hard-pressed to threaten mine again.

I also told Leslie McKenzie that I wanted a detailed, line-by-line accounting of the expenses the department was deducting from the revenue I brought in.

I didn't expect her to give it to me—and, of course, she never did—but I figured that subtly calling them on their "creative" way of producing financial statements would help put an end to the matter.

A FEW MONTHS LATER, on Wednesday night, April 22, after I'd gotten home from the hospital, I got a call that one of my patients noted a gush of fluid. I told her I'd meet her at Cornell, and I headed back across the George Washington Bridge.

Some women go through many hours of painful labor, and she was one of them. She didn't deliver until the wee hours of Friday morning. I had office hours again on Friday, so it didn't make sense to drive all the way back home to New Jersey only to have to turn around and come back a few hours later. I decided to just stay at the hospital, finish up some paperwork, and be ready for my patients when my regular office hours began on Friday morning.

Because of the warning from Leslie McKenzie, Mrs. Kiman had been filling up my schedule and I had a great number of patients that day. I dragged my sleep-deprived self from patient to patient and consultation to consultation. Between this interruption and that, I got stuck working late, as usual. Mrs. Kiman left at 4:00. I'd let the nurses go home at about 5:00.

After making notes on several charts, and getting all my patient records in order, I headed back to my office, ready to shed my lab coat, close up, and leave, at long last, after a marathon couple of days. As I walked through the door, I noticed a sheet of paper on the floor. Someone must have slipped it under my door.

Picking it up, I saw that it was from Dr. Ledger and was addressed to me.

The first thing to catch my eye was that he got my academic title wrong. The letter was addressed to "Yvonne Thornton, MD, Assistant Professor." It may seem a small thing but it stung. It suggested that, in his mind, although he had promoted me to associate professor three years before, he still couldn't see me as more than an assistant professor.

I had plenty more to be disturbed by as I got to the body of his text. His tone was scolding and rude. He wrote that the continuing deficit in my faculty practice revenues *"will not be tolerated"* and that he *"reluctantly must eliminate payment of your May and June supplemental compensation."*

He wasn't just reducing my faculty practice salary, he was going to pay me absolutely nothing for my faculty practice.

The small portion of my salary that wasn't "supplemental" was what I got paid to teach as a member of the faculty. What

Cornell labeled "supplemental compensation" was almost all of my pay.

He finished up his note with a nasty jab at my dedication: "…*your faculty plan practice activities this year indicate a lack of continued commitment to the group.*"

I hadn't seen my husband and children for days. I was ready to fall asleep on my feet after devoting the past forty-eight hours to delivering babies, taking care of patients, consulting with residents and attendings, and other professional duties. While my commitment was to my patients and the residents, all my actions benefited Cornell and its faculty practice.

Tired as I was, I forced myself to re-read the letter to see whether I could have misinterpreted its harsh tone.

No. It said what it said.

I felt a wave of nausea as the shock rolled over me. My body threatened to collapse in sobs, yet the tears wouldn't come.

I picked up the telephone and called Shearwood.

"I'm leaving," I said.

"It's about time. I haven't seen you in two or three days."

"No, Shearwood," I said, "I'm leaving this place for good. I've had enough."

Concern rushed into his voice as he asked me what had happened, and I felt my emotions release at last.

I told him everything, weeping all the while, until I was empty of tears.

"Do you want me to come pick you up, honey?" he gently asked when I was finished.

I told him, no, I was all right now. I had the car with me. I'd get myself home.

THE NEXT MORNING, Saturday, I brought the kids to the office, and packed up everything that was mine. I boxed up my medical journals. I pulled my diplomas off the walls and the family pictures off my desk, covered them in bubble wrap and tucked them away in cartons. I removed my mink covers from the stirrups in the exam rooms and took down the mobiles I'd attached to the ceiling above the exam tables. After one last look around, I left for good.

All weekend long, I wrote letters to my patients. I had to let them know that I wouldn't be coming back and I had to tell them why. I arranged for them to see a lovely young woman whom I had trained as a resident and who'd gone on to become a caring OB-GYN in private practice. In my letter to my patients, I thanked them *"for keeping me a very happy person. Because with every delivery, I knew I had held a bit of immortality in my hands."* To my friends and colleagues, I sent another explanatory letter.

And then, I answered the letter Dr. Ledger had had slipped under my office door with my own, of resignation. In the letter, I told him that I was *"tired of being disrespected in a department to which I had given my steadfast loyalty for a decade."* I enclosed my keys and ended it with this wish:

"May the future be as kind and honest to you as you have been to me."

chapter ten

Goin' Up Yonder

*"Be able to help one another, not with strain but knowing
what they was taught to do ... help your sister out."*
—DONALD THORNTON

EVERY TIME I THOUGHT of Dr. Ledger's letter, I cried.
For the next three weeks, I obsessed about what had happened and berated myself for not seeing it coming. I'd been
a fool not to recognize the impossibility of my situation at
Cornell. But another thought kept colliding with that one: what
do I do now? I had no plans and no prospects.

I didn't get the opportunity to sit alone, pondering my
future, for very long. The phone began to ring with offers from
other hospitals that wanted to set up their own perinatal centers. One call came from Long Island. Another came from a
hospital in one of New York's outer boroughs. And then I got
the call that helped me begin the healing process.

Dr. Abraham Risk, my mentor when I did my residency
at Roosevelt Hospital, was now chairman of the OB-GYN

Department at Morristown Memorial Hospital in New Jersey. He'd heard that I'd left Cornell and wanted me to join him.

"I've been trying to get you for years," he reminded me.

And I'd wanted to work with him again for years, but the timing hadn't been right. Gruff old Dr. Risk was the first person I'd contacted after leaving the military in 1982. He'd always said that, wherever I was, if I needed a position I should call him. But back then he'd just become chair at Morristown Memorial. The northern New Jersey hospital had had just a bare-basics obstetrics department. It wasn't yet a major teaching hospital and offered no perinatal services. So I would not have been able to teach if I'd joined him there, and I would not have been able to practice my maternal-fetal medicine subspecialty.

We'd kept in touch every couple years since then, but whenever he mentioned Morristown I'd always tell him that I couldn't leave Cornell. I was committed to academic medicine, research, and teaching, none of which Morristown would be able to offer me.

Much had changed since we last spoke, he said.

Morristown's nursery was no longer just a Level II facility. It was now a Level III referral center to which the smaller hospitals in the area sent their sickest mothers for treatment. It now had a neonatal ICU. And it was ready to expand into high-risk obstetrics.

"We want to be the first hospital in northwest New Jersey with a perinatal center," said Dr. Risk.

If I agreed to come to Morristown, he said, the hospital would build me a state-of-the-art diagnostic center for high-risk obstetrical patients.

It was a tempting prospect, but I had been an associate professor at Cornell. I didn't want to go to a hospital that couldn't give me an academic appointment.

Dr. Risk said that wouldn't be a problem. Morristown was affiliated with Columbia University, and its medical students and residents in affiliated teaching programs rotated through the hospital. I would be teaching those residents and medical students.

I knew that Dr. Risk would give me everything I asked for, if it was in his power.

Maybe this was finally the payoff for all my hard work, even if it was coming from an unexpected source. I agreed to meet with him to discuss the possibility of joining him at Morristown.

Outwardly, Dr. Risk had none of the polish of Dr. Ledger, but he had such depth beneath his sometimes rough exterior. In my opinion, Dr. Ledger, for all his poise, wasn't worthy to be mentioned in the same breath as my old mentor.

I fondly remembered Dr. Risk's ways from my time as a resident at Roosevelt. If you heard, *"God damn it, Jesus Christ!"* you knew the old man couldn't be far away. But beneath that crusty surface, he was the sweetest guy that you'd ever meet and a real straight shooter. Whatever he told you, that's the way it was. If you were doing something wrong, he'd tell you. If he couldn't get something for you, he'd say so and say why.

I revered the old curmudgeon.

And if I was a more caring than average physician, it was because of him and the policies he instituted at Roosevelt. The OB-GYN Department was as cutting-edge as that of any hospital in New York but, thanks to Dr. Risk and his somewhat unconventional philosophy, it also had something that very few comparable teaching hospitals of the time had: a thriving midwifery practice.

Midwives helped train the residents at Roosevelt Hospital, taking over the Labor and Delivery floor after midnight, so a patient who was admitted at 2 o'clock in the morning was first seen by a midwife instead of an obstetrical resident. Midwives Barbara Brennan, Eldra Simmons, Jeanne Kobritz, and Nancy Cuddihy introduced me to an entirely different approach to pregnancy, encouraging me to think about obstetrics as part of the natural order, not as pathology. While our professors taught us about the myriad concepts, medications, and procedures we had to understand medically and master surgically, the midwives instilled in us the understanding that we were dealing with our fellow human beings and that our empathy and humanity were every bit as important as our medical training.

They lived the true definition of "obstetrics," which means "to stand by." They were there not to interfere but to assist, and to make sure that the mothers were as comfortable and warm as possible. The perspective they gave me was probably why I felt it was my responsibility to be by a woman's side from the very beginning of labor. By contrast, many of my OB-GYN colleagues who trained elsewhere would tell the residents and nurses, "Call me when you see the head crowning."

Driving to Morristown Memorial, past acres of lush green manicured pastures and stately homes, I was reminded that Morris County was one the most affluent in New Jersey. This was horse country, where the United States Olympic Equestrian Team trained.

Goin' Up Yonder

The hospital reflected that affluence with its bright, modern façade and lobby, about as different from the stuffy, ancient feel of Cornell as it was possible to be. I almost felt as if I were walking into a high-end hotel instead of a Level III medical center.

I hadn't seen Dr. Risk in years, and yet the intervening time seemed to dissolve away as I greeted my old friend. He gave me a hug, shepherded me into his office, and asked what it would take to convince me to join his team.

As was true of most maternal-fetal medicine specialists my age, I'd had limited training in ultrasound during my perinatal fellowship. While running Madonna's New Jersey office, however, I'd gotten an immersion course in reading and interpreting ultrasound scans. I'd gone to every ultrasound symposium available. I read every book on the subject that I could. So in a way, my truncated experience with Steve Klein and Madonna Perinatal—distressing as it had been at the time—actually turned out to be one of the best things that could have happened to me.

The Madonna episode also introduced me to the best perinatal nurse on the face of the planet: Carol Ruf. I told Dr. Risk I needed Carol Ruf with me if this perinatal diagnostic center was to be everything I envisioned. I also needed a talented ultrasonographer and again, the person I selected was the same one who had worked with me at Madonna.

Cheryl Rosen was so good, she often seemed as much a magician as an ultrasonographer. I listened and learned from Cheryl as if she were one of my professors. As I did, I became confident and proficient in interpreting even the most difficult sonographic images.

Taking images of a fetus isn't as simple as imaging the heart or liver or ovaries on a stationary patient. The fetus is moving constantly, tumbling around in his or her little amniotic sac. If I asked for an image of the fetal heart, many other sonographers would say, "I can't get it. The baby's moving around too much." Cheryl would not only get that image, she'd also get all four chambers as well as the outflow tracks.

If I said, "Cheryl, we need to have a cut of the corpus callosum," Cheryl would say sure, no problem. And her scan would look as perfect as the ones in the textbooks.

In her hands, that ultrasound transducer was like a violin bow.

Dr. Risk said, whatever you need, just say the word. With that music still ringing in my ears, in August 1992 I joined Morristown Memorial Hospital and brought along Carol Ruf as my perinatal nurse and Cheryl Rosen as my ultrasonographer.

I SURVEYED THE FACILITIES and equipment that Morristown already had and made up my wish list. Unlike Leslie McKenzie, my new perinatal center administrator, Barbara Remschel, was a delight. Although the hospital had plenty of advanced technology in place, new and better diagnostic equipment was always being developed. Dr. Risk had assured me that he wanted our diagnostic center to have the best. But the best could be costly.

I was used to Cornell, where Dr. Ledger denied almost all of my requests, with the exception of a few cans of yellow paint. I almost held my breath as I told Dr. Risk that we should have a Picture Archiving and Communication System (PACS) that allowed the transfer of files digitally from one computer to another. Digital imaging was in its infancy at the time, but it was already apparent that PACS was the future. If we needed to have a consultation with an expert on, say, skeletal dysplasia or cardiac disease, and we had a PACS system, we'd be able to shoot a copy of the fetus's image to the proper specialist electronically and get a much faster response. Before PACS systems were developed, scans such as X-rays and ultrasounds had to first be developed. Then they were read by placing the film in front of a type of light box. With PACS, scans could be reviewed immediately on a monitor. And because the images were digital, we'd be able to magnify the scans on the screen, to focus on points of interest.

PACS systems cost more than $100,000.

At Cornell, I wouldn't have had a chance of getting the equipment. But this wasn't Cornell.

"If that's what you say we need," said Dr. Risk, "we'll get a PACS system."

Just like that. Anything that I believed was necessary for the new diagnostic center, we could get. I almost felt a little like Cleopatra, needing only to express a wish to have it fulfilled.

If we were going to have the best perinatal diagnostic center in New Jersey, we'd need one other piece of major equipment—an Acuson ultrasound machine—and this was even pricier than the PACS system.

Acuson ultrasound machines were top-of-the-line and provided perfect resolution. An Acuson could take an image through thick layers of fat and skin and get every angle of the fetus. Cheaper machines couldn't do that. Because I hadn't been formally trained in ultrasound, I didn't want to risk rely-ing on poor equipment. We needed the best.

I told Dr. Risk, waited a beat, and then gave him the price tag: about a quarter of a million dollars.

"That's going to be a capital expense," he said. With a capital expense, the hospital itself has to put it on its budget, not the department.

"You have to present your request to the board of directors of the hospital."

"Can't you do it?" I asked.

He said no. He knew nothing about ultrasound. "If they asked me questions, I wouldn't know what I was talking about."

I knew that other doctors from other departments would be vying for the money to get their own big-budget items. I was new at the hospital and couldn't be certain of success.

But I'd been one of the Thornton Sisters, and if I had to give a presentation, well, it was "Showtime," as Daddy would say. So I gathered my thoughts and prepared a short lecture about why we needed to have this quarter-million-dollar ultrasound machine. I put together a slide presentation to help me pres-ent the talk, and then sought out the hospital's audio-visual technician for help. During our days in the band, Daddy taught us to always check out the audio-visual equipment ahead of time to make absolutely certain that there were no glitches that would spoil the performance.

The presentations were scheduled in the Malcolm S. Forbes executive boardroom for after 6:00 p.m., and the A-V technician warned me that he wouldn't be around. No prob-lem, I said. Just show me where the slide projector is, how to control the drapes, how to control the lights, and I'll take it from there.

Everything in the boardroom was controllable from the lectern with dials and buttons.

There were three of us making our presentations to a group of about eight distinguished-looking, white-haired gentlemen who convened around the boardroom's long, sleek, mahogany conference table.

One of the gentlemen said, "Okay, we're here to listen, and at the end we'll make our decision." He added what I already knew: they could fund only one of us.

The first doctor made her pitch, handing out bound booklets with pictures and diagrams. Then it was my turn.

I got to the lectern. I lowered the shades with one button, closed the curtains with another, checked the volume on the microphone, and then hit the projector. I used my laser pointer to accentuate key points on the slides as I made my pitch. The Acuson would actually *save* us money, I said, because we'd have fewer misdiagnoses and less medical-legal exposure. At the end, I hit another set of buttons. The slide projector was turned off, the draperies slid open, the shades went up, and the lights came back on.

One of the white-haired gentlemen said he'd been attending these board meetings for about fifteen years and was so impressed that I could understand the workings of the A-V system, "My vote is that Dr. Thornton gets whatever she wants."

Where had these people been all my professional life?

I wasn't hidden away in the sub-basement. They allowed me to paint my office sorbet pink. I had windows. And now, I was getting the best diagnostic equipment that money could buy. People actually appreciated my expertise and were happy to have me.

That's not to say my situation at Morristown was problem-free. The radiology department wasn't happy about the new perinatal diagnostic center; they thought I was intruding on their turf. The local OB-GYNs resisted because the concepts were so new and I suspect they felt threatened. One went so far as to tell Carol that he and some of the other doctors were doing whatever they could to get rid of us.

"We're going to shut you down in six months," he said.

Dr. Risk said not to worry. "They're not accustomed to sending their private patients to another physician and being told what to do," he said. "So they're going to have to adapt, and that's going to take time."

I didn't let it bother me. After Cornell, I had my armor on. In Dr. Risk, I had a champion who would see to it that the attitudes of those who were unhappy about the new center didn't interfere with its mission. And I knew that despite what anybody said, we were damned good.

But contrary to Dr. Risk's predictions, the private practitioners at Morristown didn't adapt and didn't send us their patients. The local OB-GYNs essentially boycotted the perinatal center. It didn't much matter. Within a year, we had one of the premiere diagnostic centers in the New York metropolitan area. Physicians from as far away as Philadelphia and New York City sent me their high-risk patients, especially for chorionic villus sampling, knowing that I'd been a pioneer in the procedure.

We had the PACS system. We had the Acuson ultrasound machine. And we had a formidable team. The diagnostics center was thriving.

Carol Ruf, the clinical coordinator of the center, was the heart of the operation.

A charming pixie of a woman, Carol couldn't have been more than five-foot-two. She had hair so blonde it was almost white, a turned-up nose, and blue eyes that sparkled with intelligence. Carol knew more about perinatal testing than most perinatologists, and had more perinatal intuition than I've ever seen in another human being. She could just look at a patient and half the time she'd know what that patient needed. A nurse practitioner with a master's degree from Columbia, Carol had been certified in every way it was possible to be certified in perinatal nursing.

One of her key responsibilities was conducting fetal surveillance for patients whose babies were at risk of dying in utero.

During fetal surveillance, the mother relaxed in a Barca-lounger-type lounge chair while Carol hooked her up to a machine that both checked for contractions and monitored the baby's heart. Carol would give the woman a device with a push-button; each time the mom felt her baby move, she'd hit the button. Carol would then measure the baby's heart rate as it kicked. If the heart rate increased by fifteen beats above the baseline and stayed there for fifteen seconds (and if Carol got two episodes like that during the test, according to the parameters), the baby was fine and the mom could go home.

But Carol was too meticulous to assume the parameters always applied. She saw these mothers twice a week and got to know the way each fetus behaved. More than once, a clinic patient would have a poor test but confide to Carol that she hadn't eaten before her appointment. A nurse going strictly by the parameters would simply convey the results to me without further comment, and based on those test results it would be my responsibility to tell the woman's obstetrician to admit the patient for possible delivery. Carol knew, however, that when a mother was dehydrated the baby might not be as active and would seem to fail the test even if the fetus wasn't in real distress.

She'd tell me not to rush to recommend hospital admission if she knew the mother hadn't eaten. "Let me feed her a bagel and re-test her."

At first, when Carol had a hunch about the tests that didn't line up with the parameters, I was skeptical, but I soon learned to trust her instincts.

Carol would give the woman some breakfast and re-test. And lo and behold, an hour or so later the baby would be kicking up a storm; the test would be perfect.

Just as she knew when a poor test didn't mean a baby in distress, she could sense when a good test didn't mean all was well.

One patient who came in was diabetic and also noncompliant, meaning that she didn't follow recommendations to control her diabetes. Carol put the woman on the monitor, and the baby twice met the test's criteria.

Still, Carol felt something was wrong.

"It's different from all the other times this baby's been here, Dr. Thornton," she said. "I've been monitoring this baby for weeks, and I don't feel good about this."

But the baby met the criteria, I said.

She shook her head. "I know this fetus; it's not doing well."

I said, all right, if you feel that way, let's go to the next level.

So Carol pulled a portable ultrasound machine up to the lounge chair. With ultrasound she could check the amount of amniotic fluid around the baby, check how well it was breathing, and see how much—and how well—it was moving.

About a half-hour later, Carol rushed in to show me the ultrasound results. There was so little amniotic fluid around this baby that it looked like it was bound in Saran Wrap. And it wasn't breathing very well.

No other nurse I know would have realized the baby was in distress. With so little amniotic fluid, if we'd sent the mother home that day the umbilical cord would most likely have been compressed, interrupting the oxygen flow from Mom, and the baby would have had a high risk of dying in utero.

Thanks to Carol's instincts, the baby was delivered that day and was in great shape.

Like I said, we had a formidable team. And Carol Ruf was an amazing nurse.

I'D BEEN HAPPILY ENSCONCED at Morristown for about seven months when I heard that my sister, Linda, still a dentist in the Army, was going through a terrible situation with her commanding officer. Linda had been studying to become Board-certified as a prosthodontic oral surgeon. For the Boards in prosthodontics, she had to do bridgework in a patient's mouth for four days, while being tested each step of the way. It would be a grueling examination.

Linda's commanding officer (CO) didn't want to give her time to prepare for the test, despite an Army rule that said he had to. Worse, when she was casting a crown, some of the gold got lost in the machine. Thinking that Linda had stolen the gold, her commanding officer called the military police to investigate. The police immediately recognized that Linda hadn't taken the gold and that it was caught in the machine, but the commanding officer was still threatening her—and this was just one incident among many with this colonel. Linda had done two tours of duty in Korea, had served at Walter Reed in the Washington, D.C. area, and had always had an exemplary record. But since she'd been transferred to San Antonio, Texas, her commanding officer, who had indicated he didn't like women officers—especially black women officers—had made her life miserable. He threatened her with an Article 15 that would ruin her chances for promotion and effectively end her military career. An Article 15 is a trial initiated by a commanding officer if a soldier commits an offense that does not merit a formal court-martial.

She called me in tears.

"Linda, get back to work and don't worry about it," I said. "Everything will be fine."

"But he's a colonel."

I assured her that I would handle it. I'd been in the military myself and I knew how things worked.

I called my congressman, Robert Torricelli, and told him that it looked like my sister was being harassed. As a veteran myself, I understood that the only thing the military is afraid of is Congress. I also knew that Congressman Torricelli was the kind of representative who delivered when a constituent called.

Linda called me back about a week later.

She said she had been working on a patient when she heard a commotion outside her office. Generals were coming in the back door and people were standing at attention.

"These people came in with these briefcases that had the congressional seal on them and they went into the CO's office."

Linda's commanding officer had to explain everything he'd done to her. He didn't like that one bit, she said.

But after that, the colonel stopped harassing her. And he agreed to let her transfer to Walter Reed for her next tour of duty. That was still months away, but she figured she could hang in until then. The congressional investigators seemed to have unnerved him.

WOODY, NOW FOURTEEN, still had his eye on the big prize in chess: the red jacket that would identify him as a member of the All-America Chess Team.

He hadn't made the team yet but he was in Dallas with his father and sister to play his first national tournament, which could be a big step in that direction. The tournament was for high-school students and Woody was a high-school freshman; and although Kimmie was only in seventh grade, she was rated highly enough to compete in the tournament. Shearwood and I knew she probably would get bored and lose in the first round. We were used to Kimmie's whims by now. She would sometimes tag along to tournaments but not really *play.* Or else she'd play for a while, get to the point of boredom, make a blunder (either intentional or unintentional), and that would end it.

something to prove

Relentless Woody would play until 3:00 a.m. if that's what it took to win. And sometimes, that's what it took.

Woody and Kimberly wouldn't be playing against each other because they were rated differently. Kimmie, with a skill level rating of 1435, was in the under-1600 group of players. Her rating meant she was better than most other chess players in the United States (an average player is rated about 1000) but not in the rarified crowd in which Woody played. His rating was already 2115—quite an accomplishment for a high-school freshman. Grand masters, those few who achieved world championship status, were rated above 2600.

Like me, Shearwood knew little about chess, but he was a patient chaperone and made sure that the kids got what they needed, from ordering the pizzas to providing perspective when a game or match didn't turn out as well as hoped.

I was on call at Morristown Memorial over the weekend but I received regular reports from Shearwood and the kids on the tournament in Dallas.

Kimberly, apparently, had been motivated to compete, for a change. It seems that the top players got moved, after three or four rounds, beyond the velvet ropes into some very cushy seats, and the games were being broadcast in the hotel on closed-circuit TV. If the top players were getting the royal treatment, the Divine Miss Kim was going to be among them. Cameras rolling? She was in her element. Kimmie might not have been passionate about chess but she sure was passionate about the spotlight.

She loved it so much that she competed through to the end, besting player after player, all of whom were older than she was.

With the cameras focused on her, she outplayed her last opponent. Shearwood told me that not only did she win her section of the tournament, but Kimberly Itaska McClelland, my little girl, had also become the first African-American woman ever to win a national chess championship.

My baby had made history? I nearly fainted.

Woody had done extremely well too, coming in second in the highest division of the tournament against the top-ranked high-school players in the country.

All I could say was, "Wow!"

The following day, they had the kind of problem that nobody minded. Kimmie and Woody each received a humongous trophy. Tall as my kids were, the trophies must have been close to half Kimmie's height and almost half as wide. My gregarious little twelve-year-old went out into the parking area to scout for a way to transport their prizes to the airport. When she came back, she informed her father that the trophies would easily fit in a limousine—and she'd already found a limo driver with time on his hands.

We were all flying high for a couple of weeks, celebrating our two chess stars. And then I got the news that brought us all down to earth again.

Donna, my oldest sister, had lost her battle with lupus. She died on April 27, 1993, about a week shy of her forty-ninth birthday.

Although I'd been told, five years earlier, that this day was coming, it still didn't seem that it could be real. I had known that Donna was doing poorly. When I'd seen her a few months before, she'd looked weaker than ever. She'd been on oxygen and in a

wheelchair for more than a year. She had an IV for pain medication. I'd seen her decline but it just didn't register with me that
this was close to the end. Or maybe I didn't want to know.

My younger sister Linda and I spoke by phone later that
day about Donna's funeral. We sisters had been busy with husbands and careers, living separate lives in far-flung places, so
for the most part we had drifted away from the close bonds we
had as children. The exceptions were Linda and Donna. Linda
had stayed with Donna for weeks at a time while waiting to be
deployed overseas, and the two had deepened their connection.

Linda sounded heartbroken and even considered canceling
a preparatory course to help her pass her Boards. She was due
to be in Atlanta, Georgia, for the prep course that week and
under the circumstances, she didn't think she could do it.

I told her no, whatever you do, don't cancel. It could make
the difference in passing your Boards. It's what Donna would
have wanted. The funeral wasn't until the following week, so
she'd be able to get to both. Make Donna proud, I said, and
Linda finally agreed.

She'd been planning to drive from the base in San Antonio, Texas, to her course in Atlanta. She had to bring lots of
very expensive dental equipment with her, and she didn't feel
safe checking it as baggage. Driving had made sense before,
but with Donna's funeral looming Linda would have to fly
if she was to make it to both places. I told her not to worry,
that I'd pay for first-class airfare for her and a second seat for
her equipment.

With that settled we hung up, and I began making arrange-
ments for the sad trip ahead. But a little while later, I got

another call from Linda and this time, she was even more distraught than before.

She'd told her CO that her oldest sister had died and she needed leave.

Linda recounted the conversation. "He said, 'I don't care about your family. The military is your family now.'"

He refused to give her the time off.

Linda told me she went numb when she heard those words and simply got up from her seat and left without first being dismissed.

Now she worried that this colonel, who had had it in for her since she arrived in Texas, would demote her. I tried to assuage her. The Army wouldn't deny an officer the right to go to her own sister's funeral, and no commanding officer could defend such a decision, I told her. I again said not to worry. Just get done what needs to be done. It would all work out.

LINDA EVENTUALLY GOT a higher-up to reason with the colonel, who grudgingly agreed to let her go and to not "ding" her record for leaving his office without permission. I assumed the colonel's unpleasant memory of the visit from Congressman Torricelli's staff helped to bring him around. I didn't think any boss could rival Dr. Ledger for low blows, but this Texan colonel was giving it a solid try.

The funeral mass was held about a week after Donna's death, on her birthday.

The service was in a large, lovely, modern Catholic church in the Virginia suburbs. Donna had converted to Catholicism when she married Willis.

something to prove

A priest in somber vestments said mass and then, one by one, people came up and spoke about how Donna affected their lives.

When it was my turn, I talked about the Thornton Sisters and how it all began with Donna, who had asked Daddy for a saxophone when she was a little girl. I spoke about the weekends performing together and how the money from our gigs helped put us through college. I couldn't find any more words and was beginning to choke up, so I sat down and let the next Thornton sister speak. As I left the altar, I think it finally sunk in.

I would never see my big sister again.

chapter eleven

Polishing the Legacy

*"It gives me some kind of good feeling just to know
I've accomplished something."*
—DONALD THORNTON

SOMEHOW, WITH THE LOSS of both Mommy and Daddy,
and now Donna, having a book written about our family
felt more urgent than before. I again thought of Jo Coudert, who
had written our story so beautifully for *Reader's Digest*.

Jo had told me, years earlier, to give up on her; she wasn't
going to help me write the book and that was that. But Daddy
never gave up on something that was important to him, and I
was my father's daughter. I'd called Jo from time to time to see
if she'd changed her mind. She kept refusing.

One evening, after spending the day at a medical symposium in Colorado, I turned on the television in my lodge. A
movie called *The Court-Martial of Jackie Robinson* was on, and
I was immediately riveted. The story focused on the legendary
ballplayer's early years, during World War II, after he'd been

drafted into the Army and risen to the rank of lieutenant. Robinson had been stationed at Fort Hood, Texas, and had refused when a bus driver ordered him out of his seat and told him to move to the back of the bus. The situation escalated, despite a rule that Army buses were to be de-segregated. White Army officers and enlisted men sided with the bus driver, called Robinson "uppity" and a "nigger." Although he was court-martialed, he was eventually exonerated.

Watching the movie brought back memories of Daddy: the cadence of speech, his quiet dignity. Daddy had talked about the bigotry he'd encountered in the Navy during interviews he'd done with Frank Conroy in the late 1970s for the planned book about our family that never got written. That publishing offer had collapsed along with the movie deal.

As I thought back to that time, I realized I'd never mentioned those interview tapes to Jo Coudert and probably should have. Just because *I* hadn't been able to convince her to help me write a book, didn't mean that *Daddy* couldn't.

I called Jo from the hotel and told her about the interviews. "Just listen to them," I said. "That's all I'm asking you to do."

Whether she was intrigued by the thought of hearing Daddy's story in his own words or she just wanted to get me to stop nagging her I'll never know, but she agreed to let me send her the tapes. As soon as I got back to New Jersey, I did.

A woman of many talents, Jo was a watercolorist and she later told me that she played the tapes in the background as she applied her first wash of color to paper, added a glaze, and then filled the page with pastel sky, trees, and flowers. After a while though, my father's voice captured her full attention and she let her brushes idle in her water jug as she listened to him talk about growing up poor, marrying young, and developing the determination that his five daughters would rise above the circumstances into which we were born and would become doctors.

It's not that Jo didn't already know the story; she did. But I'd guessed right. Hearing it told by the man who'd done it all, and getting a firsthand sense of his intelligence and integrity, moved her in a way that all my supplications never could.

She agreed to collaborate with me on a book about my family. We met every Saturday for twelve months; and with Jo's tape recorder going, I told her everything I could about growing up in the Thornton household.

Finally, we had a sample chapter and an outline of what the rest of the book would be. Jo brought it to her literary agent, Richard Parks, who promised to submit it to all the big publishing houses. I expected the publishing world to be as moved by my father's wisdom as Jo had been.

I was about to get an education in publishing.

"I can't sell it," said Richard Parks. "I can't sell it," he repeated, as if he wanted to be sure we understood how impossible a task we'd given him in asking for him to find a publisher for this book.

He had submitted our book proposal to Simon & Schuster, Doubleday, Random House—every major publisher in New York.

Nobody wanted it.

There's no conflict, the publishers complained. It's just a story of two parents raising kids. What's the big deal?

Parks said that one publisher told him, "If Donald Thornton were a pimp and he had six prostitutes, *that*, we would buy."

something to prove

I was shocked, but Parks explained that publishing is a business and publishers want books that will make them big profits. To many publishers, that means stories that are more titillating.

"But I'll keep trying," he promised, although he didn't sound optimistic.

WOODY WAS NOW A high-school sophomore and beginning to think about his future. I'd always told my kids that they could be anything they wanted to be, as long as what they wanted to be came with an MD after their names. My parents had decided that their daughters would be doctors when we were all still little girls, and their decision had given me the fulfilling life I was living. I wanted the same for my children.

Woody had been squeamish as a little boy. Once, an episode of the TV series *ER* showed a very realistic scene of a person convulsing. Woody was so frightened by it, he refused to watch the show after that. It seemed a less-than-propitious sign for a child whose parents expected him to follow their path into medicine.

But after his friend Kevin passed away, Woody started talking to our pediatrician, Dr. Russell Asnes, about leukemia and how doctors could help sick children. Dr. Asnes took Woody under his wing and patiently answered all Woody's questions, encouraging him to think about one day going to medical school.

So I was sure that Woody had considered it. However, it wasn't until years later that I was certain he'd follow through.

I rarely took my children to work. Hospitals are full of microbes that can make kids sick, and I didn't want them exposed. One day, though, for some reason, Woody had come to Morristown Memorial Hospital and I was introducing him around to the nurses and other staff.

Woody's eye caught a group of medical students walking down the corridor and he asked me who they were. I explained that they were from Columbia on their rotation through Morristown Memorial. He seemed less interested in where they came from than their attire.

"Why do they wear short white jackets?" he asked.

I told him it had to do with the medical hierarchy. Attendings wore long lab coats. Medical students wore short white jackets. Residents and interns wore short white jackets and a white skirt or white pair of slacks.

"So they wear white jackets," he said, with the same expression on his face I recalled from the time he first saw the red All-America Chess Team jacket.

That was all he said, but I knew from that look, he was thinking, *I've got to get me one of those.*

He started asking Shearwood and me questions about going to medical school: What would he have to do? What would be the best school for pre-med? What should he be thinking about in high school if he wanted to become a doctor?

And that, of course, made his proud mother very happy.

MONTHS HAD GONE BY and the only news from our literary agent, Richard Parks, was of this or that publisher rejecting the book.

My life was full and rich. Morristown's perinatal center had a great reputation. I'd been tapped to give a speech at the opening ceremonies for the annual American College of Obstetricians and Gynecologists on a topic close to my heart—treating the whole patient, not just the pathology—and got a standing ovation from my peers. And my kids were doing well.

I told myself that this should be enough for any one person. And yet, I felt I owed it to my parents, especially Mommy, to get that book written.

I was almost ready to give up hope. Then one day, Richard Parks called with good news.

He'd submitted our sample chapter and outline to Birch Lane Press, a small house that had published Thurgood Marshall's biography, and Birch Lane Press wanted to publish our book.

I'd never heard of Birch Lane Press but I was elated. The editor, Hillel Black, saw the book as inspirational. He wanted to meet me.

We met for lunch at one of the elegant private clubs on East 43rd Street in New York City, and I liked him right away. He had an avuncular manner combined with cosmopolitan charm. He could have been Lionel Barrymore's younger brother.

And he just loved Daddy.

He put his hand on my shoulder and said, "You know, your dad was a great guy."

I told him I hoped that others would read the book and discover that too.

Jo and I worked together even harder than before; we still had just an outline and the rest of the chapters had to be written. Hillel Black was extremely supportive through the whole process, just as nice a man as you could ever hope to meet. I didn't know quite what to expect once it was finally printed and on the bookstore shelves, but I felt a great sense of accomplishment. *The Ditchdigger's Daughters* was going to be a reality.

I HAD MORE THAN a full plate, as director of the perinatal center at Morristown, and a mother of two teens, who was also working on a book.

My darling husband picked this moment to suggest that we go back to school together and get our Executive Master's degree in public health with an emphasis on Health Policy and Management.

"Shearwood, I already have more degrees than a thermometer," I said.

I was about as eager to go back to school as I was to volunteer for root canal. Shearwood, however, was gung-ho and worked hard to convince me.

"Your father always said you've got to think ahead," he reminded me. "Yvonne, this is the wave of the future."

When he invoked Daddy's name, he got my attention. I figured he was probably right.

Medicine was changing, becoming more of a business, with Health Maintenance Organizations (HMOs) and insurance companies dictating the terms. The executive MPH program had been designed to prepare doctors to navigate those changes. The traditional MPH program concentrated on epidemiology and biostatistics. The executive MPH degree added strategic management, health care finance, health law, total quality assurance, and organizational theory to that curriculum.

The more I thought about it, the more I saw the logic of

Shearwood's suggestion. I was reminded of a patient I'd seen recently, a woman in her fifties who'd come in as an emergency admission and was bleeding heavily. She had already soaked through a Turkish towel before I saw her, and the flow hadn't stopped. The woman had been hysterical—but not with concern about her hemorrhaging.

She was petrified that her insurer would refuse to pay for her medical care if she didn't first get its approval for her treatment.

"I have to get pre-certified," she insisted.

"You're hemorrhaging," I said and noted that her pulse was becoming more rapid. I begged her to just let me help but she was more afraid of an insurance claim denial.

"No, they won't pay for it," she said. She refused to sign the consent form for me to treat her until I got an authorization.

So I took off my gloves and went to the telephone to talk to the insurance company representative.

I didn't fully appreciate how risky it was to give insurers such power until I told the insurance representative that my patient had already lost 500 cc of blood

"What's 500 cc?" the insurance rep asked.

This was the person who would decide whether I could treat a hemorrhaging woman? Someone who didn't have even the most basic medical knowledge?

I explained that 500 cc was more than a pint of blood, but realized that a person who didn't already know that probably wouldn't recognize how serious the patient's condition was.

That's when I knew medicine was in trouble. No longer could physicians simply focus on the best interests of our patients. We had to first say, "May I?" to faceless know-nothings who

196

had patients so frightened that some, like this woman, would sooner risk bleeding to death than having their bank accounts bled dry due to a claim denial.

At staff meetings, too, we were being told to pay attention to an alphabet soup's worth of new insurance terms: PPO, AHP, HMO, IPA, POS, carve-out, stop-loss coverage, profit-sharing incentives.

If you weren't conversant in insurance-speak, you weren't going to get approval for the care your patient needed. The program Shearwood wanted us to attend would help us navigate these perilous waters.

"AND FOR THE FIRST time," said Shearwood, "we'll march down that commencement aisle together."

I'd graduated from medical school in 1973 and he had in 1974, so we hadn't gone through the commencement ceremony together. There was something very appealing about doing that as husband and wife. I told him I'd do it.

So there I was, forty-seven years old, slinging a book bag over my shoulder and carrying around a stack of textbooks.

I had forgotten how intense school could be—and this program was a killer. Classes met on Thursday, Friday, Saturday, and Sunday, once a month for two years. The rest of the month could easily have been gobbled up by obligations related to the coursework: studying, researching, writing papers.

What had I gotten myself into? I'd made the commitment and I would see it through, but Shearwood relished the experience.

What you have to understand about my husband is that

although he's unusually intelligent, he's typically laid back and laconic. I'd never seen him participate in group activities or volunteer his opinion without being asked. If not for his six-foot-five frame, he could easily fade into the background in almost any setting.

Not this time, though.

Every topic we covered fascinated him: health law, organizational theory, statistics, epidemiology—you name it. Whatever the subject, my Shearwood had done the analysis, related it to his experience, and come back with solid ideas.

He was like a house on fire.

He had all the paradigms put together, and everybody in the class was in awe. Here we were in a roomful of MDs from Columbia, Cornell, and other top universities. When the course first started, you could just see what they thought when they heard he was from Harlem Hospital. I caught the knowing looks that conveyed low expectations.

A few months into the course, though, Shearwood had put Harlem Hospital on the map. He was indisputably at the head of that class. I was so proud of my brilliant husband, even as I struggled to keep up with him.

MEANWHILE, WOODY HAD been racking up chess championships one after another. Kimmie had been the first in the family to win the top prize in a national chess tournament, but Woody was the one with the drive to keep winning. Woody became the highest rated Black player under age 20 in the United States. He earned title after title: U.S. Amateur East Individual Championship; National Junior High School

Co-Champion; New Jersey High School Champion; New York City Junior High School Champion; National 11th Grade Chess Champion. Woody earned eleven state championships, and all those wins helped him attain the level of National Master at the age of 15 and Life Master at the age of 17, putting him in the top one percent of all chess players. He kept going and became the first African-American to ever win more than one national championship; his record still stands.

But I suspect what meant the most to him was when he got the prize he'd been reaching for since that day when he saw the boy in the red jacket. Woody was selected from among 28,000 eligible young people to be one of the forty-one members of the All-America Chess Team. And he got his own jacket—black rather than red by the time he made the team, but with the all-important logo embroidered on the back.

KIMMIE WAS STILL AMBIVALENT about chess competitions. Her passion and competitive spirit were channeled into music. She joined the Teaneck High School Choir, then auditioned for and was accepted into the much more competitive Bergen County Choir. I should have known that with a mom who had spent her pre-teen and teen years in an all-girl band, at least one of my kids would be bitten by the music bug.

I went to every performance and applauded as loud as any-one. I knew if I discouraged her about her music, it would only make my rebellious young daughter decide to run off and sign up with the first record producer she found. So I bit my tongue and praised her as she grabbed her place in the spotlight and soaked up the accolades. All the while, I kept my fingers crossed that biology and organic chemistry would prove as intriguing to the Divine Miss Kim as a Bach cantata.

IN MARCH OF 1995, *The Ditchdigger's Daughters* was published. This book that nobody had wanted to publish began attracting readers. It didn't have a big launch, the way that mega-authors with mega-publishing houses do, but those who read it seemed to connect with it, and they told others. Word of mouth, from one reader to another, slowly built an audience.

After the unfortunate Christmas dinner meeting at the Plaza with my sisters and Phil Galdston, I'd decided not to mention this project to my sisters until it was completed. I sent each of them a copy of *The Ditchdigger's Daughters,* hot off the presses. Although it didn't quite seem possible, I swear that Jeanette and Rita were even angrier about the published book than they'd been about the prospect of Galdston authoring a book about the family. But it didn't matter. By the time they learned of it, it was a done deal.

Birch Lane Press had a very modest Public Relations department. Having been in show business, I knew that exposure was everything. So I personally commissioned a Madison Avenue public relations firm that had a very enthusiastic young publicist by the name of Jennifer Szabo. Birch Lane Press arranged a limited promotional book tour that had me going around the country for book signings. And then, as I was set to go to Dallas, the Oklahoma City bombing tragedy occurred and the rest of the tour was canceled.

I didn't mind, because I knew that Jennifer wouldn't give up and would redouble her efforts. She got the book written up in the *Wall Street Journal, The Washington Post,* and *The New York Times Book Review.* She also submitted it to be read on the nationally syndicated *Radio Reader* with Dick Estell, who reads entire books over a period of weeks on his daily radio show, which is heard all across America. She knocked on doors and made phone calls and made sure the book was in every bookstore imaginable.

One day I took her aside and said, "Jennifer, I know my mom is in heaven watching us down here, and I don't believe that the bookstore is where she really wanted this book."

I explained about her dream of having a book about our family in a library. That's where I wanted to focus our attention. I wanted to go to a school library, where children could find the book, pick it up, and with luck, become inspired to make better lives for themselves.

"You're the first author who's ever asked that," Jennifer said. Most of her authors wanted bookstores and book signings.

I understood why, but I had different priorities. I asked Jennifer if she knew of anyone with influence among the book buyers for schools and libraries.

"You need to talk to Dr. M. Jerry Weiss," she said after researching. "He knows everybody in the scholastic system."

So I called Dr. Weiss. Our first conversation didn't go well at all.

"Don't tell me you're another one of those writers who has books that you're going to sell from the trunk of your car?"

I said, no, I had no such plans. I just knew that this was a book people would want to read and I wanted to be sure that they had the opportunity, even if they couldn't afford to go out and buy their own copies. Then I told him about my mom, and he softened up a bit and promised to read the book.

When he got back to me, it was as if I were talking to an entirely different person. Jerry Weiss loved the book. He became a staunch advocate of *The Ditchdigger's Daughters,* referring to it in his talks to other university professors and helping to get it on reading lists.

Thanks to Jerry Weiss, Mommy's wish was finally granted. The book was picked up by schools and libraries throughout the country.

WOODY WAS GOING TO be a doctor, no question in my mind. Now it was just a matter of latching onto the coattails of a prestigious university so he'd have the best opportunity to shine.

He applied to Stanford, MIT, Amherst, and Georgetown, plus six Ivy League schools. It was a stretch, but being a national chess champion gave him an edge. He'd done well on his SATs. He'd maintained an A average in school.

April is the month in which schools contact kids to tell them whether they've been accepted. Early that April, Woody surprised me with a call to my office at Morristown.

"Mom, I got accepted to Yale."

"Oh, great, honey, great," I said. But he wasn't finished.

"I got accepted to Princeton, too, Dad's school."

Two of the top schools in the country and they both wanted Woody! We were thrilled. And, of course, Shearwood was excited about the prospect of his son attending his alma mater.

A few days later, Woody called me at work again.

"Mom, I got accepted to Harvard."

Harvard? Wow. "Forget about Princeton and Yale, baby, you're going to Harvard," I said.

"What will Dad say? He's going to be upset if I don't go to Princeton."

I said, we'll talk to Dad about this.

Shearwood was disappointed that Woody was snubbing his old school, there was no denying that. However, when Woody told his dad the reason, Shearwood understood completely and never said another word about Woody's choice.

"Princeton doesn't have a chess team, Dad. Harvard does. And I want to play chess."

"That's a pretty good reason to go to Harvard," said Shearwood.

As it turned out, our Woody was accepted to every school to which he applied—all the Ivies and Stanford, too.

Our little boy, almost all grown up, was on a firm course to begin the rest of his life. I had no doubt he'd do well.

I also think I understood fully, for the first time, a little of what my mother and father must have felt as my sisters and I fulfilled their dreams for us and started college. It's an indescribable sensation. You're proud and sad at the same time. Your babies are almost ready to fly on their own. You want them to soar as high and as far as their abilities can take them.

But you also want to hang on to them for a little while longer. No matter how big they are or what their accomplishments, they're your babies. Always.

Dr. Thornton, playing her sax with Fred Santiago at Battista Dance Showcase, 2007

Dr. Thornton doing the swing with partner Tom Roberts

Dr. Thornton and Tom Roberts perform the paso doble at New Jersey Fred Astaire Dance Championship, Atlantic City, 1986

Dr. Thornton and Bill Wynn cha-cha at the Grand Nationals Ballroom Championships in Miami Beach, 1991

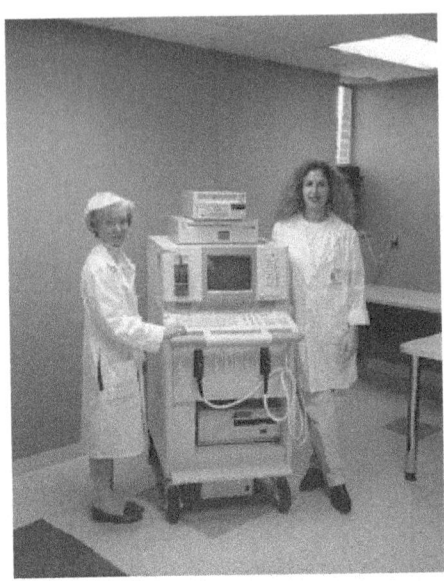

Carol Ruf, MSN, RNC and
Cheryl Rosen, sonographer
beside the Acuson machine
1992 in the Perinatal
Diagnostic Testing Center,
Morristown

Dr. Thornton as
Director of St. Luke's
Perinatal Center

Woody and Kimberly, 1993
National High School chess
champions, Dallas, Texas

Woody McClelland, proudly displaying his
All-America Chess Team jacket, 1994

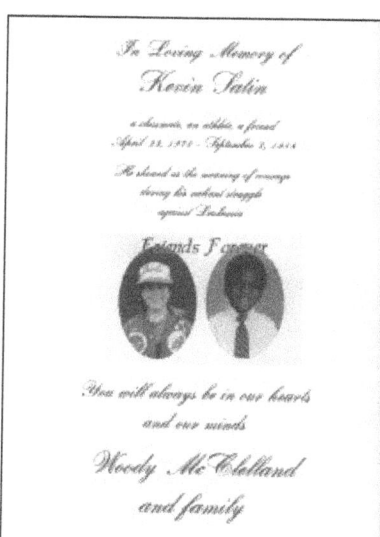

Teaneck High School yearbook, 1996—
memoriam to Kevin Satin

Woody and Kimberly show their
college pride in Harvard crimson
and Stanford cardinal

Dr. Thornton, receiving her honorary
Doctor of Science degree from
Tuskeegee University, 2003

Dr. Thornton in braces, 1997

Dr. Thornton and
Dr. McClelland,
recipient of Columbia
Alumni Federation
Gold Medal, 2005

Keeping it in the family:
Dr. Thornton, Dr. McClelland,
and Dr. Woody at Woody's
Columbia University College
of Physicians and Surgeons
graduation, 2004

chapter twelve

No Good Deed...

*"Malice wastes time that you could be doing
something positive with."*
—DONALD THORNTON

L IFE SEEMED TO BE going so well that I could almost forget the lawsuit that Helen Morris had filed against me in
1991, after she lost the baby she'd been carrying and developed
a life-threatening systemic infection. The trial was scheduled
to begin in March, 1997. Between the time she filed the
lawsuit and the trial date, massive stacks of legal documents
had been filed and hundreds of hours of attorneys' time had
been spent on the case. Since Cornell and its insurance
company handled the finances, I wasn't privy to the amounts
spent, but I knew that the costs had to be astronomical.

The attorneys at Cornell's law firm, Martin Clearwater
& Bell, continued to tell me not to worry. The attorney I met
with said he could see from the records and notes that I wasn't
at fault in any way, and neither was any other physician who

consulted on Helen's case. Everything that could have been done for Helen had been done.

"Dr. Thornton, I don't know how they got a medical expert to say that there was malpractice," he said. "I've been practicing for thirty years and this is a slam-dunk case. I think it might even be thrown out."

I felt a bit better after hearing that, and then immediately felt concerned again at his next remark.

"The only thing that bothers me is that it's going to be tried in the Bronx," he said.

I asked why that was a problem.

"Because that's plaintiff's territory."

He explained that in certain areas, such as the Bronx, juries tend to favor the plaintiff—in this case, Helen.

I reminded him that he'd said a moment before we had a slam-dunk case.

He said that that was still his view, based on the case file. "Don't worry, Dr. Thornton, we're on top of this. We've had tougher cases and we've prevailed."

I was still frightened. It was *my* reputation on the line, my entire life's work. I'd always been a conservative and careful physician. I knew that I'd done everything humanly and medically possible for Helen. I could say with certainty that she wouldn't be alive today had I not been so thorough and careful—but how she'd developed the infection that began her ordeal was still a mystery.

Would a jury, seeking a solution to this mystery, brand me as its cause?

I didn't hear from Martin, Clearwater & Bell until it was

time to go to trial. Even then, they told me I didn't have to show up until it was my turn to testify. I wondered if that made sense. Shouldn't I be there to explain matters to the attorneys if something inaccurate was said? But the attorneys saw it differently.

There was also another disturbing turn of events. The veteran attorney who had been on the case since Helen first filed her lawsuit had been assigned to a different case. His last-minute replacement, I was told, was "just as experienced," and with the evidence supporting my medical decisions and management, they felt the most senior counsel was not necessary. But I had my doubts.

You just need to be there when we ask you to come to testify about what happened, they said.

So I sat on my hands and I waited. And then, on March 20, it was my turn to go to the courthouse and tell my side of the story.

I'D NEVER PRACTICED IN the Bronx and didn't know my way around, but I followed the directions the attorneys gave me and found my way to the imposing gray building near Yankee Stadium where a jury would decide if I'd committed malpractice.

The interior was as daunting as the façade—all cold stone and linoleum. Men and women in drab suits hustled about, looking grave and purposeful. Here and there, a police officer strode by.

I felt exposed, vulnerable, as if my very presence in the courthouse was akin to guilt. I didn't know what to expect or what was expected of me.

Cornell's attorneys told me not to go into the courtroom until I was called. Instead, I waited in an anteroom out of earshot of what was being said about me.

Finally, I was brought into the courtroom and directed to the witness chair. I placed my hand on the Bible, swore that I'd tell the truth, and began answering questions from the attorney from Martin, Clearwater & Bell. The lawyer who questioned me was the substitute I'd met with earlier. He was pleasant and professional, almost academic in his approach.

Dr. Thornton, did you do this? And I answered that I had. *And did you do that?* And I said yes.

The questioning by my side was brief. The Cornell lawyer sat down at the defendant's table again, looking calm and cool, and the plaintiff's attorney stood up to question me.

I don't believe I had focused on Helen before her attorney approached me. Our eyes met but there was nothing of the camaraderie we'd once shared at Cornell. My stomach twisted a bit just seeing her and knowing what she was hoping to accomplish, but I forced myself to stay as cool as the Martin, Clearwater & Bell attorney had been.

Helen's attorney, in his dark three-piece suit, looked to be in his early fifties. His body language was that of a pugilist— cocksure, shoulders tight, hand gestures quick and jabbing. His voice shouted testosterone even when he spoke softly.

He was a man who enjoyed a fight, I could see that before he opened his mouth to ask the first question. He would destroy me if I let him. I resolved not to let him, to remain composed, and to answer his questions as I would those of a medical student.

He threw questions at me like punches, each one meant to knock me down.

Why did you do this? Why did you do that? Why'd you put that suture in there?

I answered him as I would any person who needed to understand the ins and outs of a medical procedure but he tried to twist my every word to make me appear incompetent.

Isn't it true, he asked, that you could have done a simpler form of the cervical cerclage? And I answered that in Helen's case, with her history of infection, the simpler procedure would have been riskier. With her history of infection, it was best to bury the stitches and the knot to limit the risk of wicking bacteria into the womb. I said that despite taking those precautions, it appeared that Helen had still retained some bacteria from her earlier infection—too little to show up on lab reports but apparently enough to spread through her body in a chain reaction.

He demanded to know why we hadn't done more lab tests and I explained that that wasn't the standard of care. If you have negative cultures for infection, you presume that it's negative. You don't continue to test for something that your laboratory has determined isn't there.

He barely let me finish one answer before he jumped on me with another question, each one sounding like a sneering accusation. Why did we do the procedure at thirteen weeks and not earlier? Or later? If the jury box had been filled with people who understood medicine, my answers would have made perfect sense. But these weren't doctors or nurses and this lawyer made my every move sound suspect.

something to prove

I forced myself to breathe. I refused to let this lawyer's increasingly histrionic attacks elicit an equivalent response in me. I kept my responses professional. Was I ready to turn into a blubbering bowl of jelly? As close as I'd ever come. But I wouldn't let it happen. I would not let him do it to me.

Couldn't you have done another procedure rather than rip out her uterus? he asked.

I did not rip out her uterus, I said. Her uterus had lost the ability to contract. She was bleeding to death. I could stand by and let her die or I could take out her uterus to save her life.

I began to explain that any doctor in that position would do the same, but he cut me off.

You can't talk of anybody else in your situation, he said. You're the only one who's on trial here.

I'd seen my share of courtroom dramas in the movies and on television; I kept expecting my attorneys to jump up and shout, "Objection."

I don't recall them doing so, not even once. They sat there calmly in their three-piece suits, looking unflappable as I was being flayed alive.

Couldn't you have clamped this? asked Helen's attorney and I answered, we did. *And couldn't you have tried that?* And I answered that we'd done that too.

Here is a woman in the prime of her life, not able ever to have children again, he said.

And I said, I know that. But she's here. She's alive. And she wouldn't be if I'd made a different decision. The choices were to let Helen hemorrhage to death, or take out the organ that was causing the hemorrhage.

I spoke of my reluctance when forced to do the hysterectomy, because I knew Helen, and I knew her history. I knew she wanted a baby. But she couldn't have one if I let her die on the operating table. I had to do what I did to save her life.

With facial expressions and gestures, like an actor mugging for the audience, Helen's lawyer conveyed contempt for my responses to the jury. And then he dismissed me.

The judge said, "You can stand down." And I did.

I'd done my best to explain the medical complexities but I couldn't be sure that the jury understood. How could they when Helen's lawyer twisted my every word almost before it left my mouth?

I felt like the criminal incompetent he'd tried to paint me as being.

A few days later, I learned the verdict. The jury found me at fault and ordered Cornell to pay half a million dollars to Helen.

Shock and disbelief were my first reactions. I was inconsolable.

"We'll appeal," said the attorney. But the goal of the appeal would be to reduce the award, not to clear my name.

I had not harmed Helen. I'd saved her life—yet my name would go into the National Practitioner Data Bank as someone who had committed malpractice.

chapter thirteen

Mystery Solved

"You can't hate a person; you can hate the things they do or the ideas they have, but not as a person themselves."
—DONALD THORNTON

THE MALPRACTICE VERDICT WOUNDED me in a way I can't quite explain. Knowing that I'd done everything I should have or could have to help Helen didn't change that. A part of me would never recover from the experience.

I planted a smile on my face and pretended nothing was wrong. I had responsibilities that couldn't be postponed while I dealt with the blow.

KIMMIE WAS A SENIOR in high school and ready to choose a college. I hoped she would select a school nearby but instead, she was leaning toward Stanford.

My only daughter wanted to go to a school three thousand miles away. I asked Shearwood to talk her out of it. She can go to Wellesley, I said.

He wouldn't commit to discouraging her choice. "We should just wait and see," he said.

So Kimmie and Shearwood flew out to Palo Alto, California, for a pre-freshman weekend, and Shearwood came back sold on the school.

"It's where Chelsea Clinton is going," he said.

Who cared where Chelsea Clinton was going? I didn't want my baby to be so far away. I tried to get Kimberly to change her mind but she was no help at all. "Whatever Daddy says, Mom."

So it was settled. And I was a nervous wreck.

I worried about her being so far from me. I worried that someone would take advantage of an innocent, vulnerable young woman, all alone for the first time in her life. I worried about California's earthquakes. I worried so much you'd think she had decided to go to school in a war zone—but she was my little girl and if she wasn't close by, I couldn't protect her. I prayed like life itself depended on it, down on my knees, asking God to please keep my baby safe.

I HAD FEWER WORRIES about Woody, who was about to begin his third year at Harvard. His school was close enough so he could come home every weekend if he wanted to. And Woody had always been more measured and cautious in his approach to life than his sister.

That Labor Day weekend in 1998, before college was to begin again, Woody had a big chess tournament scheduled. It was for the New Jersey State title, and Woody was the defending champion. Although Woody had won it the year before, at just nineteen years of age, he hadn't been the favorite. The fellow who had been expected to best him in 1997 was back to challenge Woody for the championship, and this time many chess aficionados were certain he'd beat Woody, even though Woody had become the United States Junior Open Chess Champion.

Unbeknownst to many, Woody had a powerful incentive to do well. The tournament started on a Saturday and ended on Labor Day, September 7, 1998, the tenth anniversary of his boyhood friend Kevin Satin's death.

"Whatever money I win, assuming I play well enough to actually win money," said Woody, "I'm going to donate it to the Tomorrow's Children Fund."

Tomorrow's Children was the charity that had raised the money for Kevin to go to Iowa to get his bone marrow transplant. If Woody could help Tomorrow's Children help another child, he felt that that would be the greatest achievement of his chess career.

I didn't say anything because I didn't want to jinx him, but I wondered whether that challenger had a snowball's chance. When my son is determined, he can do anything.

ON THE MORNING OF the final day of the six-round tournament, Woody was in the lead after five rounds. He'd won so easily and quickly that he had almost four hours to kill before his final games.

And that's when he nearly lost it all.

Shearwood and Woody decided to drive home and relax before the final round, just a half-hour away on the New Jersey Turnpike. However, on their way back to the tournament, they got stuck in bumper-to-bumper traffic. An accident had jammed up the highway. As cars in front of theirs lurched forward and stopped again, they measured their progress in inches.

Woody was getting nervous because according to chess rules, any player who is more than an hour late automatically loses. There seemed to be no way to get back to the tournament in time until Shearwood spied a parallel road on the turnpike for trucks, buses, and cars that had just been re-opened by the turnpike police and looked clear. It was as if the Red Sea had parted. As they whizzed down the highway, watching the log jam of cars on the parallel thruway, Shearwood and Woody were virtually the only ones on this newly opened road.

Quickly exiting the highway, Shearwood got Woody back with only minutes to spare to play the last round.

Woody won, not just the title again, but six hundred dollars. It was his biggest chess prize ever. And, as planned, he donated his winnings to Tomorrow's Children, in loving memory of Kevin Satin.

I WAS SO THRILLED for my son, I could almost stop worrying about my daughter. Almost. Then I saw her packing for college and went weak in the knees.

Shearwood accompanied Kimmie on the preliminary trip to Stanford. When he saw her name and that of her roommate on the dormitory door, he called right away.

"Yvonne, Kimmie is rooming with somebody named Starr. Do you think it's *that* Starr?"

"*That* Starr," would be Kenneth Starr, the independent counsel who was constantly making headlines. Originally appointed to look into President Bill Clinton's dealings with a real estate venture called Whitewater, Starr had since expanded his investigation to cover many other allegations—the latest being the president's affair with White House intern, Monica Lewinski. The investigation seemed to be getting more attention than anything else Clinton had done as president. And yes, we soon discovered, Kenneth Starr's daughter, Carolyn, was going to be rooming with Kimberly.

Because of her father's prominence, Carolyn Starr got the star treatment from the federal government. Whether it was by FBI agents or Deputy U.S. Marshals, Carolyn and Kimmie, their mail, and any visitors to their room were subjected to scrutiny. The modest dorm room might as well have been the Oval Office, with all the cameras placed in hallways and doorways outside to monitor visitors.

"Mommy, I can't even go the bathroom without having a camera pointed at me," my daughter complained.

Kimmie's protests aside, it would be almost impossible to get better security than what Carolyn Starr—and by extension, her roommate—got, twenty-four hours per day. I figured that the Big Guy had heard this nervous mom and was protecting my baby.

DESPITE THE VERDICT in Helen's lawsuit, I was gaining recognition—not just at Morristown, but also beyond. That past year, I'd been given one of the highest honors that any OB-GYN can receive. One of the directors of the American Board of Obstetrics and Gynecology had seen me being interviewed by Dr. Nancy Snyderman on *Good Morning America,* liked my answers, and, after checking into my background, decided I had the right credentials to become an oral Board examiner.

Of the 43,000 obstetricians and gynecologists in the United States, only 300 are invited to become oral examiners—physicians who determine whether candidates meet the criteria to become Board-certified in obstetrics and gynecology.

Those 300 physicians are, by necessity, among the most accomplished OB-GYNs in the country, but nobody talks about being a Board examiner, and it's difficult to learn which physicians have made it into that rarified group. The American Board doesn't publish the names. And that led to an interesting encounter. The first time I arrived in Chicago to examine candidates, I walked onto the elevator in The Westin Hotel with several other Board examiners and found myself face-to-face with Morrie Druzin. He looked startled to see me among the crème de la crème. I could understand his surprise. In past decades, examiners had been not only exclusively white but also exclusively male. I was the first Board examiner to be a woman of color. All I could do was smile.

MY PROFESSIONAL LIFE had been going well at Morristown Memorial Hospital, too, although I had to contend with the sometimes openly hostile attitude of some of Morristown's private practitioners. But now, Dr. Risk was retiring. With my champion gone, I knew things would change, and probably not for the better.

Candidates to replace Dr. Risk as chair had to interview with me, so I saw a lot of old friends and other people that I knew in the arena of perinatal medicine. Although I hadn't applied for Dr. Risk's position at first, I realized that I was as qualified as any of the other candidates, perhaps more so. I had my executive MPH in health policy and management from Columbia and I already knew the department.

A search firm had been commissioned to help find Morristown's next departmental chair and when I offered my résumé to the firm for consideration, the woman who interviewed me gushed with encouragement. I left feeling optimistic. But almost immediately, the hospital disbanded its search committee, fired the search firm, and asked the gynecological oncologist on staff to take over as interim chair while it kept looking. Whoever those in charge hoped to recruit as their next chairman, it seemed that I wasn't it.

While I wasn't privy to the inner workings, I gathered that there was a struggle between those who wanted Morristown to continue as a teaching hospital and those who preferred to abandon teaching, which brought prestige but not profit.

By the following year, 1999, the position still hadn't been filled.

Without a permanent chairman to sign off on equipment purchases or National Institutes of Health (NIH) grants, progress in the perinatal center came to a halt. I started looking for a different position.

I received an offer in early 2000, but not as a result of my own search efforts. Instead, a letter arrived from the president of St. Luke's-Roosevelt Hospital in New York City, Sig Ackerman, who said he'd seen me mentioned in a newspaper article and noticed I'd trained at Roosevelt.

I was often quoted in the media thanks to the success of

The Ditchdigger's Daughters; and following that success, Jo Coudert and I had also co-authored a book on women's health, which brought me more media attention.

Dr. Ackerman said he was in the process of developing a new OB-GYN department with a new chair who would be arriving from San Antonio, Texas. He asked me to contact this new chair and tell him that Roosevelt's president had sent me because he wanted me aboard as part of the new obstetrical faculty.

Some of my fondest memories were of Roosevelt, and not just because of Dr. Risk and his progressive policies. The entire faculty hierarchy had been very forward-looking, committed to the best in patient care and the highest ethical standards. Being a resident at Roosevelt taught me what was important in medicine. In a very real sense, those lessons still guided me as a physician.

I called the new chairman, Dr. Oded Langer, and agreed to meet him at the New York Obstetrical Society for a quick interview. He wasn't someone I'd come across professionally. Curious about his background, I did a bit of research. An OB-GYN from Israel, Langer had spent two years in South Africa during the 1980s, a time when apartheid was the law of that country and black South Africans had been stripped of their citizenship. He had completed a fellowship in Maternal-Fetal Medicine, but never became Board-certified in the subspecialty. Dr. Langer had published some articles on diabetes and one seminal paper on the treatment of diabetes in pregnancy with an oral agent instead of insulin. That seemed to be it.

I was surprised that Roosevelt had chosen someone as chair with credentials that were, to my eye, relatively thin, but

I reserved judgment. I had applied for the position of OB-GYN chair at Roosevelt Hospital several years earlier, but was never given the courtesy of a reply.

Now, I arrived at the elegant wood-paneled New York Obstetrical Society for our interview, introduced myself, sat across from the rather stout new Roosevelt chair who spoke with a very thick accent, and could immediately tell that nobody had mentioned to Dr. Langer that I was black. The way he looked at me—after a lifetime of living in this skin, I knew the look—it seemed apparent he was less than thrilled to invite me onto his faculty staff.

"Builds character, Cookie, builds character," Daddy had always said, whenever I confided about the bias I faced at work. I wondered how much more character I needed to build at this point.

I took strength from the memory of my father's words, but given Dr. Langer's reaction, I realized if I returned to Roosevelt I would have to prove my worth all over again. I also knew that two issues weighed in my favor: the president of the hospital had asked me to join the faculty, and I was an expert in chorionic villus sampling. Regardless of Dr. Langer's personal reaction to me, I had a lot to offer. He needed me, and we both knew it.

I wasn't all that excited about working for a chairman whose credentials couldn't approach my own and who was less than welcoming. Still, I knew it was time to move on. Morristown had finally chosen a permanent chairman, one of the private practitioners. He was neither an academic nor particularly interested in focusing on academics. I'd wither if I stayed put. This was my chance to get back into New York City as an academic. I decided to accept the offer, signed a two-year contract, and came on faculty in May of 2000 as one of Roosevelt's new perinatologists. I would be one of six new maternal-fetal medicine specialists hired by Dr. Langer. His mandate was to make Roosevelt Hospital the leader in perinatal medicine in New York City.

ROOSEVELT HAD CHANGED from the hospital I remembered. The major difference had happened soon after I'd completed my residency; Roosevelt had merged with St. Luke's Hospital. Each maintained its separate campus, Roosevelt at 59th Street and Tenth Avenue; and St. Luke's in upper Manhattan, near Columbia University at 114th Street. Both were under the aegis of the medical school, Columbia University College of Physicians and Surgeons, as affiliate teaching hospitals.

After a recent major renovation, the hospital also looked different. When I'd been a resident in 1973, Roosevelt had been a modest medical center that served the community. Now, it had a new façade with a soaring triple-arched stone entry and imposing columns. It even had a new address, although the building was in the same place. No longer was it 428 West 59th Street. Roosevelt was now officially located at 1000 Tenth Avenue.

IT BECAME APPARENT rather quickly that Dr. Langer was no Dr. Risk. A career-centered administrative taskmaster, he expected his faculty to work long hours and do double duty at St. Luke's as well as Roosevelt. With both of my kids in college the hours were somewhat easier on me than would have been the case in earlier years, but the schedule was still brutal.

I was just getting acclimated to the new environment, furnishing my new office, and becoming acquainted with my new colleagues when I got a call from one of the circulating OR nurses who had assisted in Helen Morris' surgery back in 1988. Everybody has different duties when a patient comes to the operating room, whether it's the anesthesiologist, the surgeon, or the nurses. The scrub nurse, for example, makes sure all the instruments are on the table properly. Another nurse preps the patient by using an antibacterial solution to disinfect the part of the body on which the surgeon will be operating—in Helen's case, the vagina. This had been the duty of my caller, the former circulating nurse.

Other than a Christmas card every year, I hadn't heard from the nurse since I'd left Cornell, more than eight years earlier. She told me she'd retired.

"But this has been on my mind for so many years, and I just need to talk to you," she said.

She paused for a moment and then continued: "I forgot to do the vaginal prep for Helen."

I was too stunned to speak. Time slowed and I was back in the operating room in 1988. I remembered telling Helen everything would be all right as she drifted off under the anesthetic. I remembered the care I took in stitching the cerclage. I could recall almost every moment of the surgery. How could I forget, when it had haunted me for twelve years?

The vagina is teeming with microscopic organisms. When these bugs mind their own business, they're actually beneficial; but when you're doing surgery, you want them gone. Otherwise, they can multiply and cause a nasty infection.

Helen's vagina had never been disinfected and because of that, Helen almost died. Her ordeal had nothing to do with anything that I had done or failed to do. It was simple negligence by the circulating nurse.

I should have felt vindicated but it was too late for that. At least the nurse's confession answered the question that had dogged me for twelve years: *What had gone wrong?*

All the care I'd taken to ensure a successful procedure, all the preparation, had been for nothing. With one seemingly small omission, many lives had been damaged—and one life, that of Helen's baby, had been lost.

I don't know what, if anything, I said in response to the nurse's confession.

I just felt numb.

Why had she waited all those years to tell me, years she must have realized I'd spent soul-searching, questioning every action, second-guessing every decision I made?

By the time I got home that night, I was reeling as her revelation sunk in. I cried and railed to Shearwood. The lawyers had to have spoken to her, I said. She knew I was being sued for something that was her fault. How, I asked Shearwood, could she have kept silent for so long?

He listened calmly until I was finished then he put his arms around me.

"What are you going to do now, dear?" he asked in his soothing baritone. You could scream at her, he said, accuse her of cowardice, make demands—but to what end?

"It's good to know what really happened, Yvonne, but now you have to move on."

My husband has always had a calming influence on me. Although a very different man from my father, Shearwood, in his way, was just as wise.

He was right, I knew. There was nothing more to do except to say, "Mystery solved" and leave it in the past. The pain would linger a while longer; the scar was there forever. The time for action though, was over.

LATER THAT MONTH Woody graduated from Harvard, on the same day as his parents' wedding anniversary. It was a joyous moment. Although he hadn't attended his father's alma mater, Princeton, in the fall he would be going to the same medical school that both Shearwood and I attended, Columbia University College of Physicians and Surgeons.

Kimberly had yet to find her calling. Her original plan was to major in biology at Stanford. Shearwood and I had chanted the mantra to her since she was small: "pre-med...pre-med... pre-med," and this would have been her first step. Her adviser at Stanford, however, insisted she "lacked the mental capacity" for the sciences, for reasons never explained. Her grades certainly said otherwise. I tried to nudge her back toward science.

"Don't listen to the adviser, honey," I said. "Do what you want to do."

Kimmie said that that was the problem. She didn't know what she wanted to do. She decided to be an English major, mostly because she didn't need an adviser to sign off on the choice, but she never took an English class. With her penchant for science, she switched next to mechanical engineering. That seemed to be going well, especially since her product design classes allowed her to use her creative side, until one of her professors gave her a new assignment: design an ergonomic toothbrush handle. She realized what her life would be if she stayed in product design: creating incremental changes in mundane products and seeing her work become obsolete within a year. When Kimmie puts her heart into something, it has to be something with a future. She gave up product design and chose studio art as her next major.

Not exactly pre-med.

Still, she was barely out of her teens and I knew it had to be stressful making life-changing decisions while living so far from home. I bit my tongue.

The one constant in her academic life was her music. She'd joined an a cappella group called Talisman during her freshman year at Stanford and quickly became its leader. The group, which sang everything from old African-American spirituals to international folk tunes, headed to South Africa to perform during the summer recess to honor the memory of a Stanford student and anti-apartheid activist, Amy Biehl, who had been slain there in 1993.

About the last place on earth that I could imagine wanting to go as a black woman was South Africa. I feared for my child in that place where apartheid had so recently been the law of the land.

My headstrong daughter, though, would not be dissuaded.

Warily, I cheered her on when she called from Cape Town to report on her adventures. Her enthusiasm bubbled through the transatlantic phone lines as she told me how the local blacks cried with joy when they heard this group of twenty American college students, of black, white, and Asian descent, singing in their native Zulu. It was a language that white South Africans almost never learned—and that many of the country's whites probably felt was beneath them to utter.

Talisman sang in Cape Town's schools, visited the township's churches, and performed on its streets. It was a moving experience for Kimberly. In her calls home she spoke of the songs of freedom and black pride that they sang, and the warmth of the local people. It meant a great deal to her to be there.

As for me? I wasn't at ease again until late June when she was safely back home.

chapter fourteen

A Colossal Prayer

"Never dread anything. Just go ahead and do it."
—ITASKER FRANCES THORNTON

I'D GOTTEN SOMEWHAT MORE than I bargained for when I signed on as Roosevelt Hospital's senior perinatologist. Dr. Langer also named me as the director of the St. Luke's Hospital Perinatal Center. I spent three days a week at the uptown hospital and two days at Roosevelt. Like all Roosevelt faculty physicians, I taught residents, interns, and medical students. I was on call for emergencies and covered Labor and Delivery as well. If I sometimes felt like a gerbil racing on a wheel to nowhere, I was grateful that I didn't have a private practice on top of my other responsibilities.

One Friday afternoon at 5:00, after putting in a full day at St. Luke's at 114th Street, I was ready to go home to New Jersey. St. Luke's was convenient to the George Washington Bridge, which was just north of West 168th Street.

something to prove

I was on call that night for Roosevelt Hospital—the physician who would be contacted in case of emergency. As I was leaving, a fellow perinatal attending at Roosevelt Hospital phoned to say, "Transfer of care," meaning that he was signing off, and informing me (the attending coming on-call) of the patients on the floor and on Labor and Delivery.

I asked him to give me the particulars on the patients on L&D.

"Everything is okay, Yvonne," he said. "We just have one patient but she's not in labor."

The patient had ruptured her membranes and had been there for three days, he said. They were just observing, using conservative management until either she got a fever, she went into labor, or the baby's heartbeat indicated trouble.

Nothing to worry about for now, he insisted.

On the surface, this sounded like a run-of-the-mill non-emergency situation where you simply wait for nature to take its course. After so many years as a physician though, I'd developed a sixth sense about mothers and babies. Or maybe it was something in what the attending said—or didn't say. I sensed that I should postpone my commute home and trek down to Roosevelt instead.

THE WONDERFUL THING about Roosevelt Hospital was that some of the secretaries, medical clerks, and nurses had been working there for thirty years or more. When I returned to the hospital after being gone for decades, some of them remembered me from when I was a resident.

"Oh, Dr. Thornton, you're back. How are you doing?"

A Colossal Prayer

One of these women, Mrs. Williams, was the medical clerk in Labor and Delivery. She was responsible for keeping track of records such as vital birth statistics: the time and date of each baby's birth, what type of delivery, and the outcome of each birth.

She asked why I was there on a Friday night and I told her I was on call, and the attending had mentioned a patient whom I felt I needed to see for myself.

"Oh, *that* patient," she said, and pointed me to the room where Mrs. Jackson had spent the last three days.

I put on a white coat, went in to check on her, and got the surprise of my life. Lying like a little whale in the bed was 545-pound Mrs. Jackson. Beautiful face, beautiful temperament, but immense.

I called in one of the nurses and asked if Mrs. Jackson had had a fever; she said no. I checked the chart and noticed that the patient had a previous cesarean delivery.

Then my eye caught the fetal heart rate strip. It was totally flat.

"How long has it been since someone looked at the fetal heart rate monitor tracing?" I asked.

"The day attending on L&D said it's a little flat, but it's okay," answered the nurse. "That was about an hour ago."

"It's not okay," I told the nurse. With ruptured membranes, and a flat fetal heart rate tracing, this baby could be in trouble.

I slowly backed out of the room and thought, *Oh, my God, what do I do now?* There was only one thing I could do, but the surgery was fraught with potential complications. The mother could die on the table because of her massive body weight.

231

"We need to get this baby out of there,"

"To be honest with you, nobody wanted to do the cesarean because she's so heavy," the nurse confided. "When she was first admitted, we had to take her down on the loading dock to weigh her."

The other attending should have delivered the baby when he saw that fetal heart monitor strip. Instead, he had quietly slipped away and made Mrs. Jackson my problem.

Out at the reception area, with a wave of her hand, Mrs. Williams motioned me to her desk.

For the past three days, doctors had been running in and out of that room, she told me. "There's a reason why you came down here. When I saw you, I knew that God had sent you just for this patient."

I wished I could say I shared Mrs. Williams' optimism. One thing we could agree upon: I would need divine intervention in order to successfully operate on this mom and her baby.

Her panniculus—that massive apron of fat that began at her waistline and draped down to her lower body—extended to her knees. When delivering a morbidly obese woman like Mrs. Jackson, there are no good options. Many surgeons would begin their cut above her navel in an attempt to avoid that enormous layer of fat, while trying to find the uterus to get the baby out. Other surgeons would just cut through the several inches of abdominal fat in an attempt to gain access to the uterus. But I had found that the safest way to get to the uterus and perform cesarean deliveries in obese women was to make the skin incision low in the exposed "bikini" area, after lifting up the apron of fat toward the patient's head. In cutting through layers and

232

layers of fat and flesh to get to the lower part of the uterus, a surgeon could cut too deeply and inadvertently injure the bladder, causing significant damage; or could accidentally cut an artery, leading to a massive loss of blood. Because these unfortunate complications had recently occurred on the obstetrical service in normal-sized patients, I understood why the attending wanted to be as far away as possible when Mrs. Jackson was wheeled into the operating room.

The technical difficulty was daunting.

I called in the anesthesiologist; he walked into the room and looked at our patient, and I could see the intense concentration in his face as he worked out the complexities in his head.

We batted our concerns back and forth. Would we need two OR tables, shoved together, or would that be more troublesome because the tables could separate during surgery?

Two tables could cause more problems than they solved. We agreed on one large table.

Epidural, spinal, or general anesthesia? With an epidural, we'd have to try to sit the patient up and put the anesthetic through a small catheter in her back. It meant, again, finding a way through masses of flesh. But with an epidural, the anesthesiologist could keep pumping in anesthetic as needed for hours at a time. It might take me hours to get through to the baby. It would be safer for the mother to be awake for that amount of time, especially with someone who was already compromised by mounds of flesh. Spinal anesthesia entailed navigating through the thick layers of fat in the patient's back, and giving the anesthetic directly without the need to thread a catheter. The only drawback was that the surgery needed to be quick and not last more than an hour. General anesthesia involved inserting a breathing tube and putting the patient to sleep on a respirator; that could be difficult for a massively obese lady who had a very short neck.

After much deliberation, the anesthesiologist said he'd try the epidural. "But if I can't thread the catheter, I'll have to resort to a spinal. And that means you will need to be quick, Dr. Thornton." He got the longest needle available.

The surgical team looks to the surgeon to take the lead; I couldn't show any signs of weakness. I put on my best "Dr. Thornton in charge" face and told everyone to get ready while I went to scrub. I made a detour into the supply room where the sutures, IV poles, and other necessary OR equipment were kept.

Once alone, I paced back and forth in the narrow space. I must have been in there for at least ten minutes while the team was setting up and running around.

I silently prayed: *Please, God, you have to help me. Guide my hands. Please don't let anything happen to this mother or her baby.*

I repeated my prayer, over and over, until out of nowhere I heard a voice speak these words:

"All right, already!"

I swear the voice sounded irritated. But I knew I wouldn't be in there alone.

"Okay," I said. "I'm ready."

I got my sutures and instruments, finished scrubbing up, and walked into the OR, the picture of assurance.

With some difficulty placing the epidural, the anesthesiologist had to administer the spinal anesthetic instead. I knew the countdown had begun.

I had done some research many years before and published a paper on a technique for delivering morbidly obese patients. My earlier patients might have been, on average, half Mrs. Jackson's size, but the technique had worked on patients weighing up to 500 pounds.

"Okay," I said. "We're going to reposition all of this excess flesh and fat up toward her head, tape it up, then run the tape over her shoulders." With the fat out of our way, I explained, we'd expose her pubic area.

The area above the pubis, even in a morbidly obese woman, is usually flat and firm. Instead of a vertical incision from the navel down, I'd lift up the apron of fat and do a horizontal incision just above the pubis. That would allow me to get into the uterus and get the baby out.

"Oh, no, she won't be able to breathe," said the anesthesiologist.

I reassured him that I had done "Thornton suspenders" before. "She's accustomed to carrying around this excess weight, and it should take only about an hour to perform the surgery." If need be, I said, we could always shift her position.

EVEN UNDER THE SURGICAL masks I could detect skeptical expressions, but the surgeon sets the rules and that's what we did. We taped the patient's massive belly to her chest and swabbed her with an antiseptic solution, and I went in. I was able to perform the cesarean quickly, without incident or excessive bleeding, and delivered the baby in only a few minutes,

Amazingly, despite the flat-lined fetal heart monitor strip, Mrs. Jackson's baby girl was in great shape. Her Apgar scores—measuring Appearance, Pulse, Grimace, Activity, and Respiration—were nine out of ten.

We'd done it. After the baby was delivered and under the warmer, the rest of the surgery went very smoothly. There was relatively little bleeding and Mom was awake and breathing well.

As I left the OR, I heard the surgical team behind me, applauding. I had my own applause to deliver, but I needed to do it in private.

Back in the supply room, I got down on my knees and said, "Thank you."

Mrs. Jackson and her baby were fine and expected to go home in just three days.

chapter fifteen

Biding My Time

With woody studying medicine at Columbia College of Physicians and Surgeons—or P&S, as faculty and alumni fondly called it—my parents' determination that their children should grow up to be doctors evolved from impossible dream to family tradition. Woody was not only attending the same medical school that Shearwood and I had, he was also living in the same building at Columbia Medical Center Tower apartments that we had when he was born in 1978. Although Woody had set off to follow his parents' path, he had proven his worth all by himself, first as a chess champion and then as a *cum laude* graduate of Harvard.

Woody still had some surprises for us, though. Everyone expected him to become a pediatrician. That was the specialty he spoke of whenever he talked of becoming a doctor.

His desire to help other kids like his boyhood friend Kevin Satin seemed to be a primary impetus for his interest in medicine, and his mentor had been our family pediatrician, Dr. Asnes.

Woody came home to Teaneck for the Christmas holidays and—wouldn't you know it?—on December 26, 2000, we woke up shivering with cold. Our entire home heating system had malfunctioned overnight.

Shearwood, Kimmie, and I had just one objective: get the repairman over to the house to get that heater working again. Woody came out of his room, smiling broadly, seemingly unconcerned that the inside temperature was dropping by the minute and would soon match the wintry weather outside.

"Mom, I'm going to be a neurosurgeon," he said, as he sat at the breakfast table.

He'd been in bed, praying, he said, and had asked if pediatrics was the right choice or if the Lord had some other plan for him.

Woody insisted he got an answer, loud and clear: "He said, 'Neurosurgery.'"

Some might scoff, but I'd had my own conversations with the Big Guy. If Woody said that God had chosen a different specialty for him, I wasn't about to argue.

Neurosurgery is one of the most difficult specialties and one of the most competitive. I knew, though, that if my son set his mind on something, there would be no stopping him. And if he believed he had a calling—and he did—then we were going to have a neurosurgeon in the family, no matter how much competition there was for the few coveted residencies.

It never hurts to have a strategy, even if you have a calling, so to give him an edge, I suggested he get involved with research. Most medical students don't think of research. But I'd been on admission committees for medical school, and on selection committees for residency programs. I knew that when we would go into committee to discuss candidates, one of the first questions that would come up was, "How much research has this person done?"

So that first year, Woody began doing clinical research at the Neurological Institute. His professors were so impressed with his laser-like accuracy and hand-eye coordination that they kept Woody on as one of their collaborators.

I SAW MY SON'S future filled with possibilities, but was starting to feel less sanguine about my own prospects.

At a monthly departmental staff meeting that Dr. Langer held in the hospital boardroom, he lambasted the ten or so of us physicians in the OB-GYN Department.

The department wasn't generating enough revenue, said Dr. Langer, glaring at the faculty staff gathered around the conference table.

From now on, he said, "Everybody on faculty is going to have a private practice."

I was already shuttling between the perinatal centers at the two hospitals and teaching medical students, interns, and residents. My weekends were regularly interrupted by emergency calls. Now, he expected me to have a private practice, too?

I was pondering how to respond when the chairman preempted any rebuttal. He didn't want to hear any whining, he said. He expected us to do what he told us to do, and go where he told us to go.

"You are my property," he proclaimed.

Sitting next to me was another faculty physician who also happened to be of color. I looked at him; he looked at me. *Did Dr. Langer just say what I thought he said?*

Dr. Langer was a native of Israel, so maybe he didn't understand how such a comment would sound to someone like me, a descendant of American slaves. It didn't go over well with any of the other highly trained specialists around the table either, no matter what their backgrounds.

I flashed back to how different Roosevelt's Department of Obstetrics and Gynecology had once been. During my residency, when Dr. Thomas Dillon had chaired the department, faculty meetings were all about patient care. The distinguished and eloquent Dr. Dillon had been, at the time, president of the New York Obstetrical Society and often brought in equally distinguished physicians to speak at faculty conferences. Dr. Langer, by contrast, could point to little that distinguished his career; and whatever characteristics someone might ascribe to him, eloquence was unlikely to be among them.

Dr. Langer didn't value what physicians like Dr. Dillon valued, either. A few months earlier, when I'd told Langer that I had to go to Dallas for a week to be a Board examiner, his round face turned pomegranate red.

"You're not going," he said.

I knew he wasn't Board-certified in any subspecialty, so I tried to explain that my serving in this capacity brought honor and prestige to Roosevelt and, by extension, to him. Any other chair would be thrilled to have an examiner on faculty, I said. Langer wasn't impressed. He said if I wanted to go, fine, but he'd deduct the week spent in Dallas from my vacation time.

I'd grown accustomed to Langer speaking more like a businessman than a physician, and thought that nothing he said could surprise me. But with his "You are my property" pronouncement, the businessman was now hauling out the shackles.

Tension shot around the conference table like an electric current. None of us had signed up for this. I was obliged to stay until May, 2002 due to the contract I had signed upon joining the department. I'd barely finished decorating my office, and already I was calculating how many months were left before I could reclaim my freedom.

Glancing around the table at the expressions on my colleagues' faces, I guessed that I wasn't the only one who'd begun counting off time.

chapter sixteen

They're Not Coming

*"Love is taught, hate is taught. I've taught my kids
to love, to understand people."*

—DONALD THORNTON

T UESDAY MORNINGS AT ROOSEVELT were devoted
to Grand Rounds, starting at 7:00 a.m. This three-hour
conference was an intellectually challenging medical teaching and learning marathon in which we'd introduce and be
introduced to new concepts and new ideas. It had been like
this at every teaching hospital through my entire career as an
academic and I loved it.

On this sunny September morning, the agenda began, as
always, with a guest speaker; I believe the topic might have
been gynecological oncology. Faculty physicians, nurses,
medical students, residents, and others gathered in the auditorium to hear the speaker share his expertise. We then
took about a fifteen-minute break until 8:00 a.m. when we
held our weekly morbidity and mortality (M&M) conference,

to discuss cases that had been managed over the previous seven days.

As was standard practice for the M&M conference, one of the senior residents presented an obstetrics case, and the attendings in the audience questioned the resident about case management decisions: *How did you arrive at your diagnosis of the patient?... What literature supports your mode of management?... Why did you alter the original treatment plan?*

Typically, it was a good grilling but it kept residents on their toes and helped everyone—presenter and audience member—make better choices in patient care.

Sitting for that long, posteriors begin to get numb, so we took another short break to get coffee and other refreshments outside the auditorium before a second resident presented a gynecological case.

The halls were all abuzz at the break. At first I couldn't tell what the excitement was about. People looked alarmed and were chattering in small groups.

I stopped a nurse and asked, "Why the commotion?"

A helicopter had crashed in downtown Manhattan, she said. How on earth? We'd had helicopter crashes in Manhattan before. One copter collided with the Pan Am building back when I was a resident, and I remembered at least two other incidents where helicopters had crashed into the Hudson and East Rivers.

Everyone was sharing what was known, but nobody knew much. From bits and pieces of conversation, I gathered that it was a small plane and not a chopper that had accidentally flown into one of the World Trade Center buildings downtown.

No pilot could have survived such an impact. I hoped that no one inside the building was injured.

With the break almost over, I grabbed my orange juice and returned to the auditorium. The resident who was to present his case next leafed through his notes, ready to begin, when someone rushed through the doors and announced that a second plane had crashed into the World Trade Center towers.

A second plane? That couldn't be an accident.

All thoughts of the conference abandoned, we scrambled out of the large room and into the hallway. Somebody tuned a waiting-room television to a news channel. Surrounded by colleagues and strangers, I stared up at the small screen, attempting to absorb what we were witnessing.

Black smoke poured from the top of one tower as the television station replayed footage of a plane flying directly into the other tower. Red and orange flames exploded outward in a massive fireball that engulfed several stories of the skyscraper.

Time stopped. Nothing seemed real. If people were talking around me, I didn't hear them. With a sort of tunnel vision that permitted only the television screen to register on my consciousness, I watched, stunned and shaken. Even as I watched it happen, my mind wasn't completely understanding what was taking place, yet I stood there, transfixed. Over and over, the TV station replayed that clip. Slow motion. Close-up. With commentary. Without.

Details trickled out and played across the screen. These weren't small planes but jumbo passenger jets that had been hijacked by extremists for a suicide mission.

something to prove

The news anchor brought the world up to date to the extent possible.

At approximately 8:46 a.m., American Airlines Flight 11, en route from Boston to Los Angeles, crashed into the World Trade Center's North tower, taking out most of the ninety-second through ninety-eighth floors. Full of fuel, the plane exploded on impact. Less than twenty minutes later, at about 9:03 a.m., United Airlines Flight 175, also on its way to Los Angeles, sliced through the seventy-eighth through the eighty-fourth floors of the South tower at a slight angle, creating a sky-high inferno of massive proportions.

I tried to call Shearwood at Harlem Hospital, about four miles north of Roosevelt and far from the attacks. Unable to get through, I tried and reached Woody at his apartment near Columbia. I had no reason to believe that he was anywhere near downtown, but when the world is crashing down around you, you need to make sure. I needed to be sure. Kimmie was in Hawaii, visiting a friend. I understood that she was as distant from the danger as anyone could be and still be in the United States, but I wouldn't feel on solid ground until I'd heard from all the people I loved and knew they were safe.

The phone lines were jammed.

The attack wasn't yet over. Within about a half-hour, at 9:37 a.m., another jetliner, American Airlines Flight 77, crashed into the Pentagon.

No one knew if more planes might have been commandeered by terrorists or if the next wave of attacks might take a different form. Information was sketchy. The news anchor reported that all flights across the United States had been grounded. All New York City bridges and tunnels had been ordered closed to traffic. Chaos reigned.

I thought back to the time when I was a young girl in high school, right before my Sweet 16 birthday, sitting in Latin class, and our teacher interrupted our studies to tell us that President John F. Kennedy had been shot by an assassin. It was the middle of the Cold War and we immediately assumed the shooting was the work of the Russians. Sounding almost like radio static, whispers filled the air in the classroom: the Soviets were going to bomb us, right where we sat. We looked out the school's windows to the skies, convinced that they were coming and there was nothing we could do to stop them.

The confusion and terror of this morning was very much like that day almost forty years earlier. Instead of one horrible event though, this was attack after attack, all within the span of an hour. We didn't know the extent of it or when it would end.

People trapped on the upper floors of the towers stood on window ledges, fires raging behind them. As we watched, one after another threw themselves from the ledges to escape the inferno.

A woman reporter turned toward a thud behind her, and the camera zoomed to the hood of a car. It was covered by the bloody body parts of someone who had leapt from one of the towers. The reporter became hysterical.

I'd performed hundreds of surgeries and was accustomed to the sight of blood and guts, but no experience can prepare you for such images.

And more was to come. Just as the time ticked to the 10:00

hour, the TV screen focused on a scene that seemed surreal, unimaginable, even considering what had preceded it.

It was almost as if the South tower, one of the world's two tallest buildings, had grown weary of the effort to keep upright; it began crumbling onto itself.

People raced in all directions, screaming, crying, wailing. Sirens shrieked but their usually alarming call barely registered in the cacophony. Glass, metal, concrete, and other debris rained onto the streets. Paper enough for a hundred ticker-tape parades fluttered upward, suspended in clouds of gray-black dust.

Through the television's small speakers, the imploding tower emitted a chorus of explosive boom, boom, boom sounds before it heaved a protracted groan and roar.

Thousands of people had been in that building. Parents, wives, husbands, sons, daughters. How many had gotten out in time? How many survived?

Like all of us who lived through those awful first hours, I felt—everyone felt—so utterly helpless. And we had no way to know if it was over yet.

If I felt as if I were teetering at the edge of an abyss; what pulled me back was a call from the emergency room's head nurse.

If you're not in the operating room, she said, come down to the ER.

Firefighters and police had been leading the injured from the buildings, were still shepherding survivors from the tower that was yet standing, and would be scouring the scene of the collapsed tower for survivors. In a disaster this great, there could be thousands in need of treatment. The hospitals downtown will fill up quickly, she said, and then they'll bring the overflow of survivors to us.

All cities have emergency plans in the event of catastrophe. When hospitals near "ground zero" of a catastrophic event fill up, casualties are next brought to hospitals farther from the scene of the emergency. Roosevelt was about five miles north of these attacks. With a disaster this enormous, in the coming hours we'd almost certainly be called upon to assist; when we reached capacity, the injured would be transported to hospitals even farther uptown.

In a way, the call was a godsend. I needed to be useful. None of us could change what had happened but we could help save lives. I joined several other physicians who were mobilized by the call. We poured in from all over the hospital, wanting to be of help, until there were more doctors than patients in the ER.

Roosevelt had not yet received any casualties from the World Trade Center site. People were coming in with the usual complaints that the emergency room treats—chest pains or injuries from minor accidents.

As we waited to be called on to treat the survivors whom we were certain would soon be on their way to us, we continued to watch the coverage on a television in the emergency department's doctors' lounge.

I began to think of what we might be facing as physicians. The burns, I knew from watching the television reports, would be horrific. We had a burn unit at the ready. There would be cases of smoke inhalation. Many of the survivors were likely to have been hit by falling debris. There would be crushed limbs and internal injuries. Although I'd spent my professional life caring for pregnant women, I'd been in the military and the military trains you to be ready for anything. I could feel the adrenaline pumping through my system. I would apply my skills as a surgeon where they were needed.

And then the North tower groaned and followed the South tower in collapse.

IN THE DOCTORS' LOUNGE, we waited and milled around. How many had police and firefighters gotten out of the towers before they fell? It was impossible to know. Were survivors trapped in the rubble? Maybe. We'd all read about how, after earthquakes, people were found in pockets under ruined buildings, hours or even days after the event, sometimes with only minor injuries. There was still hope. There had to be.

But the clock ticked on and the doors through which paramedics should have begun to bring in the casualties stayed closed.

So many thousands of people had been in the twin towers. They couldn't all have been treated in the downtown emergency rooms. Where were they?

I'd lost all sense of time. All I knew for certain was that we had been waiting in the doctors' lounge for hours, when a doctor—I believe it was the emergency room chief—came into the lounge to address the physicians waiting there.

Grim-faced, he said what each of us knew by then but hadn't been willing to admit to ourselves.

"They're not coming. There aren't going to be any more survivors."

They're Not Coming

The downtown hospitals wouldn't need our help with the overflow because there was no overflow. Not enough people had gotten out alive.

Even after watching the video footage and hearing the reports, that was the news that crushed us.

I FINALLY GOT IN touch with Shearwood. He was stuck in Harlem. I told him I'd try to get back home to Teaneck and that if I couldn't, I'd stay overnight at the hospital. Woody had offered to let us stay with him at his West 168th Street apartment, but the four roommates were already crammed in there like sardines. I left Roosevelt at the end of the day, uncertain of how far I would get because the bridges were closed to traffic.

Out in the street, I was surprised to see no evidence of the choking smoke or dust that blotted out the sun in the images I'd watched all day on television. We must have been too far from the epicenter. The sky in midtown was a cloudless bright blue. That seemed wrong somehow, juxtaposed against everything that had occurred, but a whiff of the air gave hints of what the clear blue hid; it was tainted by an acrid smell I attributed to the tragedy, blown north by the wind.

All the stereotypes you've heard about New Yorkers being a lively, smart-alecky, fast-talking bunch are true ... but that wasn't true on this day. People were afraid. You could see the fear in their eyes, and it almost seemed that if you kept on looking you would see right through to their souls. These feisty city denizens, usually so purposeful and self-assured, walked along West 59th Street staring blankly ahead like zombies.

251

something to prove

I got in my car and headed toward the George Washington Bridge, fully expecting to be turned back at the roadblocks, but the police saw my MD plates and let me pass. Mine was one of the few cars that was allowed access to the bridge.

Most everyone else walked. I'd never noticed before that there was a pedestrian walkway on the George Washington Bridge, probably because no one ever used it. Although it spans the picturesque Hudson River, it isn't the sort of bridge that welcomes someone out for a stroll. One of the world's busiest suspension bridges, the fourteen lanes of its upper and lower decks are typically clogged with stop-and-go traffic. The slow parade of eighteen-wheelers spewing diesel exhaust inhibits driving with the windows open, let alone walking alongside those choking fumes. Tempers can flare during the frequent traffic jams, encouraging honking, the yelling of expletives, and rude hand gestures.

But what was true of the George Washington Bridge on any other occasion wasn't true on this day.

The walkways were packed with people trying to make it home from New York—there must have been thousands of pedestrians—and the fourteen traffic lanes were virtually empty.

Everyone was polite. Everyone walked deliberately and slowly. If New York was a war zone, the people crossing the bridge appeared to be refugees, stoically, silently putting one foot in front of the other. As I drove past, with the entire roadway to myself, the faces I scanned of the walkers looked weary but otherwise bland. I expected to see horror etched into everyone's expressions but it was as if the attack had been too much for these walkers to process.

252

They're Not Coming

We were a people in shock. It would take time simply to accept the enormity of what had happened to us, let alone deal with it.

THE CITY WAS STILL effectively shut down the following day, but my MD license plates helped me get past the police and other security forces that patrolled the bridges, tunnels, and streets and back to Roosevelt Hospital. I had patients to see. I was a physician and could not be deterred. I put on a brave face, a professional front. But I was also a human being; I was no more immune to what had happened than anyone else.

Weeks went by. The city slowly came back to life and all seemed almost to be as before, at least on the surface. We learned of a fourth hijacked airliner, United Airlines Flight 93, aimed at Washington, D.C., that was probably meant to crash into the White House or maybe the Capitol building. Its passengers had learned of the earlier hijackings and attacks on New York and Washington from loved ones they called by cell phone. They banded together to overcome the terrorists, thwarting them from reaching their target. Like the passengers on the other three hijacked jetliners, and so many who were trapped in the towers and the Pentagon, all of those United Flight 93 passengers had died—but who knew how many other lives they had saved?

I HAD BEEN PLANNING to leave Roosevelt once my contract was up. After the terrorist attacks I decided that maybe it was time to leave medicine altogether. I had fulfilled my parents' dreams and then some. For almost 30 years I'd had a "scripperscrap" around my neck. I'd delivered over five thousand babies and assisted in delivering ten thousand more.

I had published papers, had taught the next generation of doctors, and was among the oral Board examiners who grilled—and certified—new obstetricians taking their Board exams. I'd accomplished everything I'd set out to do.

Well, all right, not quite everything. I'd knocked against academe's damned glass ceiling but had never broken through to the next level. I had never been granted the title of full professor.

Still, Kimmie would be graduating from Stanford in 2002 and that would be the end of paying tuition. I could afford to relax and live the life of a pampered orthopedic surgeon's wife. After spending most of my adult life tethered to one hospital or another by a pager and later a cell phone, I could have my weekends to myself.

I gave Dr. Oded Langer my letter of resignation in February 2002. I'd leave when my contract was up in May.

A FEW MONTHS BEFORE my planned departure, I received a call from Wayne Cohen, who was chairman of Obstetrics and Gynecology at New York City's Jamaica Hospital.

Wayne had spoken at our Grand Rounds a few months earlier, and we'd crossed paths over the years many times before.

He had heard that my contract was up in May.

"I am desperately looking for a vice-chair," he said. He wanted me to take the position and also to be his Director of Maternal-Fetal Medicine.

I didn't say yes, but didn't rule it out, either, agreeing to meet him at Jamaica Hospital.

They're Not Coming

My first impression was not positive. Everything about the place said drab and dreary. The walls were unadorned cinder blocks painted white. Queens, New York, one of the outer boroughs of New York City, is the most diverse county in the United States, with large immigrant populations from India, Africa, Asia, and Central and South America. Jamaica Hospital looked like what it was: a safety net, no-frills hospital that served these mostly poor immigrants.

But when I toured the office, people were pleasant enough. Jamaica didn't perfume its waiting rooms with ambiance spray, nor was the décor elegant, but when you get past that, medicine is medicine and pregnant women are pregnant women. They needed the same care as the socialites of Park Avenue or Morristown.

Wayne and I spoke for hours. I liked him, and he liked me. I wasn't ready to say yes, but I told him I'd think about it. The offer was tempting. Here I was, a Board examiner, but I'd never been Director of Maternal-Fetal Medicine. I'd never been a vice-chair. And there was one more title I'd never held, and that was the one that meant the most to me.

I needed to have an academic appointment, I told him.

He said, "No problem." Jamaica Hospital was affiliated with Cornell. In earlier years, I would have balked when I heard Cornell. But Dr. Ledger was no longer chairman and Dr. Frank Chervenak, whom Ledger had elevated to Director of Maternal-Fetal Medicine over me, had taken his place.

I'm not coming in as an associate professor, I told Wayne Cohen. I want full professorship. Full professorship. Now, if you can do that for me...

something to prove

I CAME ON FACULTY as vice-chair in July of 2002, but the glass ceiling didn't break all the way until April, 2003. That's when I officially received my academic appointment: full Professor of Clinical Obstetrics and Gynecology at the Weill-Cornell University Medical College.

chapter seventeen

Picking Up the Mantle

"When it comes to my children, my wife,
they could ask me for the world and I would
give it to them or die trying."
—DONALD THORNTON

O N MAY 19, 2004, the roads were slick and the rain kept coming, pummeling everything and limiting visibility as I drove. The weather complicated matters because I had so much to get done, in the widely separated boroughs of New York City, in a very short span of time. I had patients to visit at Jamaica Hospital in Queens; I also had a mountain of paperwork to attend to. The in-box could probably wait another day for the necessary attention, but tomorrow's heap of paperwork would double the stack.

I had just one important event on my mind, which made it imperative for me to get to Manhattan before 9:00 that morning. This was Woody's day, the day he was to graduate from Columbia University College of Physicians and Surgeons. And it was also my day, a moment I'd dreamed of and planned for since he was a small child, when I'd held him and cooed to him about his future life in medicine in much the way my parents had talked to me about becoming a doctor.

The night before, my sister Linda, who had since retired from the Army with the rank of Lieutenant Colonel, had arrived from Lumberton, New Jersey; she and Kimmie were going to head to the ceremonies together. Shearwood, with his own hospital duties to fulfill, planned to arrive separately. My sisters Jeanette and Rita couldn't make it; they'd missed Woody's graduation from Harvard as well, but nothing, neither absent family members or the pouring rain, could dampen my happiness this morning.

Columbia holds two ceremonies for graduates: the first one on the main campus at West 116th Street for the entire Columbia University graduating class—English, engineering, chemistry, architecture, the College of Medicine, and every other discipline—and another, smaller ceremony, further uptown in the Columbia Presbyterian Medical Center courtyard, for the medical school graduates.

New York City is known for its busy, congested streets. But within the decorative black iron fencing that runs along much of Columbia's perimeter, the campus has a surprisingly serene, open feel. Majestic old brick and stone buildings, looking as if they could have been plucked from the great cities of Europe, are separated by wide green spaces and cobblestoned paths. Bronze and stone statues dot the landscape. Walking across Low Plaza, up the expansive stone steps of Columbia's granite-domed Low Library and past its ten massive, fluted, Ionic columns, you could almost forget that this campus inhabits a small pocket in the jam-packed Upper West Side of Manhattan, where every square inch of real estate comes at a premium.

On this rainy morning, however, as I drove the clogged city streets, it seemed I wouldn't get anywhere near Columbia's Low Library where the first graduation ceremony was to be held.

Thousands of people had descended on the campus for the commencement.

Just two years earlier I'd practiced at St. Luke's Hospital, right next to the campus, and I still had a mental list of all the parking garages in the area. I threaded my car through the thick traffic, stopping at several garages. All the spaces were filled. Even my own secret parking space was occupied.

Up one street, down the next, I hunted for a spot to squeeze into, my blood pressure rising as I thought, I'm going to be late for Woody.

No. That was unthinkable.

I knew of just one other place where I could park my car: outside the Emergency Room entrance of St. Luke's Hospital, a block or two from the campus. I'd probably get towed, but I didn't care. Let them take it. My son wasn't going to graduate without me. I parked, left my old St. Luke's–Roosevelt Hospital badge on the dashboard, and walked to the Low Library Plaza. The commencement ceremonies were about to begin.

The graduates were positioned on the steps and the lectern was in the center, in front of the Alma Mater statue, a large bronze of a seated goddess, representing wisdom and learning.

Guests sat in chairs farther down in the quadrangle,

facing the graduating class. Kimmie had negotiated some great seats for us, right in the front row. I don't know how she did it, but Kimmie has a way with people and I figured she must have charmed a few of the campus police officers who handled crowd control.

Umbrellas up, Shearwood, Kimberly, Linda, and I watched as speakers rose and sat, until finally, Woody came out with the Class of 2004, College of Physicians and Surgeons.

"Will the class stand," said Dean Gerald D. Fishbach from the lectern.

"Bow your heads in accession," he instructed them, then led Woody and his class in swearing to the Hippocratic oath.

"I swear by Apollo the Physician and Asclepius and Hygieia and Panaceia and all the gods, and goddesses, making them my witnesses, that I will fulfill according to my ability and judgment this oath and this covenant..."

WITH THE FIRST CEREMONY over, we scurried to our cars for the drive uptown to the second one. To my surprise, my car was right where I'd left it, next to St. Luke's ER entrance.

The courtyard gardens of Columbia Presbyterian, on West 168th Street, were covered with a massive tent. Although this ceremony would be smaller, our group became larger. Ms. Grace Rivera, Woody's guidance counselor from Teaneck High School, had come to see him graduate; as had our dear family friend Pearl Eccles, who was a labor and delivery nurse back when I was still a unmarried resident at Roosevelt.

As we strolled amid the flowers and statuettes in the garden, I found myself thinking back to May 16, 1973, and my own graduation from P&S. I could picture Mommy and Daddy so clearly, it was as if they were standing there with me again.

They were a formidable pair to have as parents. And yet they were unassuming people. All my life, they'd told me, keep going, just keep going. It doesn't matter that you came from Long Branch. It doesn't matter that you're black. It doesn't matter that you're a woman. If this is the goal that you want to reach, this is the goal that you should aim for.

And when we arrived together on that day, thirty-one years earlier, in this same courtyard, it wasn't just my goal that had been reached, it was theirs, and it wasn't just my success we were celebrating.

Daddy hadn't known anybody when he arrived that day, but he treated everyone he met like an old friend, shaking every hand he could grab hold of, and telling professors and other parents about me, his newly minted graduate.

"Did you know my baby was born here?" Daddy said to anyone who would listen. "And now, she's graduating from here."

"Daddy, you're embarrassing me," I complained.

My exuberant father ignored my pleas for restraint.

He shook the dean's hand, boasting all the while, "Yeah, that's my baby, right there, that's Cookie, that's my daughter."

Daddy looked especially dapper that day, too. He never wore anything particularly dressy, but for my graduation, Daddy donned a suit and a tie. A few years earlier he'd bought Mommy a mink stole, and she wore it proudly to my big event, never mind that this was a bright, sunny day in late spring and the temperatures must have been near seventy. If it was a day for celebration—and what day could be more so?—it was a day for that mink stole.

I don't think I'd ever seen my parents happier.

And now, as I waited for Woody to appear, I understood exactly how Mommy and Daddy must have felt.

KIMMIE ORGANIZED EVERYTHING at the uptown ceremony, just as she had on the main campus, finding great seats for our small but proud group. She'd brought her camcorder to capture every moment.

While the commencement on West 116th Street included everyone graduating from every one of Columbia's schools, at this ceremony there were probably no more than 150 graduates.

We squeezed into the aisle and sat on our wooden folding chairs, lined up in rows behind those for the graduating class.

The PhD candidates were called to the dais first, and as each name was announced, a student accepted his or her diploma, shook the dean's hand, then walked off the stage and sat again.

At last, it was the medical school graduates' turn.

As they were about to begin, the Dean of Students made an announcement from the dais.

Parents who were alumni of the College of Physicians and Surgeons, she said, would be given the opportunity to present the diplomas to their graduating sons and daughters.

Shearwood and I were taken by surprise. This was apparently a longstanding P&S tradition but since neither of us had parents who were alumni, we hadn't known of it.

Students accepted their diplomas in alphabetical order. We

waited as the Bs and Cs were called and then, as we heard the Ls, Shearwood and I made our way into the aisle.

"Shearwood McClelland, III, MD," announced the dean, and Woody walked up to the dais from one side while we entered the stage from the other, meeting in the middle. The Dean of Students handed the document in its portfolio to Shearwood as I stood to Shearwood's right.

Maybe it was the wind, or a trick of imagination brought on by emotion, but as I placed my hand over Shearwood's, I sensed my father's hands covering mine. And then, together, we extended the diploma to Woody.

Everything since Woody was born came rushing back to me in that moment, like a movie fast-forwarding through time—the Pampers and the crying and the walking the floors late at night and the snotty noses and all the encouragement speeches.

You can do it, honey, come on, Woody, I'm here for you, just like my Daddy was for me.

And as we walked together off the stage, I swear I could hear Daddy's voice.

"You done good, Cookie. You done good."

AND SO IT SEEMS I have come full circle, despite the setbacks and the challenges of being a woman who followed her heart and became a physician, who loved her best friend and became a wife, and who wanted a family and became a mother. Like an acrobat on a high wire, I had balanced career and parenthood. Now, with Woody becoming a doctor, the entire struggle was well worth it.

something to prove

But life is a continuum and there are those who will invariably doubt your worth. For people like me who want to follow their dreams and support the dreams of their children, I know there will always be something to prove.

epilogue

ALTHOUGH I HAD ESTABLISHED a scholarship years earlier
in the names of my parents at Columbia University College of
Physicians and Surgeons, The Donald E. and Itasker F. Thornton Memorial Scholarship, I knew it would never be enough to
compensate for Mommy's greatest regret. From the time she
was a little girl, she'd had big plans. She was going to graduate
from college and become a teacher. The dream seemed within
her reach until her senior year, in 1941, when she was forced
to quit Bluefield State Teachers College, after three years as
an A student, because seniors weren't allowed to work in the
school's kitchen. That's where she'd earned the money to pay
tuition until then: scouring pots and scrubbing floors.

After she became a mother, she worked just as hard to give
her daughters the educational opportunities she'd lost.

I had long tried to get Mommy the degree that poverty
had held just beyond her reach when she was a young woman.

epilogue

Finally, in May of 2005, working with college administrators and the West Virginia Higher Education Policy Commission, I secured that elusive "sheepskin." Mommy is now listed among the graduates of the Class of 2005 at Bluefield State College. I was asked to be their commencement speaker and accepted the diploma and doctoral hood on her behalf. Itasker F. Edmonds Thornton was posthumously awarded the honorary degree of Doctor of Humanities. Her diploma reads, *"She dared to dream great things and, through those whose lives she touched, great things were achieved."*

As for the rest of the family...

Woody, as I knew he would, beat out the competition for one of those coveted neurosurgery residencies. With more than thirty peer-reviewed articles under his name—an unusually large number for a resident—Woody plans a career in academia so he can continue with his research.

Kimberly received her Masters degree in Public Health from Columbia in 2008 and, to her parents' shock and delight, applied to and recently was accepted into medical school. Her caring and intelligence will make her a wonderful physician.

My darling husband, Shearwood, is still at Harlem Hospital, where he is the Director of the Orthopedics Department.

As for me, I left Jamaica Hospital in 2005 and am now Clinical Professor of Obstetrics and Gynecology at New York Medical College in Westchester County, New York. Yes, *full* professor here as well (there's no way to patch up the cracks in that glass ceiling now).

The heart-stopping moments I've spent in the delivery room and the OR over the years have strengthened my faith both in God and in womankind. There is nothing more humbling than to work to save a life and know, when you're done and the procedure is a success, that it wasn't you at all but someone much greater who was responsible. There is nothing more satisfying than hearing from a patient, many years later, that her baby who, but for a quick intervention and a lot of luck, would have been lost, just made the fifth-grade honor roll. I've kept in touch with so many of the women I've cared for as patients, and they are like extended family. I've watched the babies I've delivered mature into outstanding young men and women. They remind me of why I became a physician.

Almost none of this would have been possible if not for the determination, wisdom, and love of a man who, although a high school dropout, was one of the smartest people I have ever known: my father, Donald Thornton. More than twenty-five years after his death, Donald Thornton is still the most powerful force in our lives.

DADDY, IF YOU'RE WATCHING *from above (and I know you are), I hope you're proud of us, and of all you've accomplished through us. Love, Cookie*

acknowledgments

I WOULD LIKE TO take this opportunity to express my gratitude to those who were instrumental in making this paperback version of my book become a reality.

First, I would like to thank Patty Shannon of The Wordstation, Ltd., who worked tirelessly in transcribing the hours and hours of interviews; Anita Bartholomew, my co-author, whose perspicacity introduced me to a different perspective for the book; Jack Myers, a literary colleague who was instrumental in updating the book to its present electronic and paperback formats. And last but not least, my lovely daughter, Dr. Kimberly Itaska McClelland, MD, MPH, MBA who took time away from her busy schedule to review the entire manuscript and even assist in naming some chapters.

Thank you all.

About the Authors

YVONNE S. THORNTON, MD, MPH is an Emeritus Professor of Obstetrics and Gynecology and a double Board-certified specialist in obstetrics, gynecology, and maternal-fetal medicine (high-risk obstetrics) at New York Medical College in Westchester, New York. She is a former departmental Vice-Chair of Obstetrics and Gynecology and has personally delivered more than 5,000 babies in her career while overseeing or supervising more than 12,000 deliveries. She is married to an orthopedic surgeon and is the mother of two children, who are both physicians.

She is the author of *The Ditchdigger's Daughters*, her memoir about growing up in a poor family with parents who were determined to see all their daughters rise above their and become doctors; and *Inside Information for Women*, a health guide that answers many questions women have about their bodies from someone who's been on both sides of the stirrups.

During her 45-year career in medicine, she has conducted research at The Rockefeller University, the National Institutes of Health Pregnancy Research Branch, the National Naval Medical Center, the Naval Medical

Research Institute, and New York Hospital–Cornell Medical Center. She is the author or co-author of more than a twenty scientific papers. Dr. Thornton has become a leading authority on obesity in pregnancy and she also serves as a reviewer for the American Journal of Obstetrics and Gynecology. She received her MD from Columbia University College of Physicians and Surgeons in New York City and her Master of Public Health in Health Policy and Management from the Mailman School of Public Health at Columbia University.

Recently, Dr. Thornton was the recipient of the "LIVING LEGEND" award given by the Joseph Henry Tyler, Jr. chapter of The National Medical Association. In its 250th year, Dr. Thornton was the honored recipient of the Virginia Kneeland Frantz award for Distinguished Women in Medicine—the highest recognition for an alumna of Columbia University College of Physicians and Surgeons.

About the Collaborative Author

Anita Bartholomew has worked in publishing in various roles for more than 15 years. She was a longtime contributing editor for *Reader's Digest*; has been an editorial consultant and book doctor for numerous works of fiction and non-fiction; and, as a ghostwriter, co-authored a historical novel for an independent film company.